History of the Wars by Procopius

The Persian War. Book I & II

Procopius of Caesarea was born in approximately 500. He is generally considered to be the last major historian of the ancient world. His works have given us a unique and intimate account both of the Roman Military and its Emperor Justinian.

A native of Caesarea in Palaestina Prima little else is known of his early life, and apart from assuming that he would have received a classical Greek Education the rest is deduction rather than based on known facts.

In 527, the first year of Eastern Roman Emperor Justinian I's reign, he became the adsessor (legal adviser) for Belisarius, Justinian's chief military commander who was then starting out on what would become a brilliant military career, initially in the East of the Empire. After early successes Belisarius was defeated in 531 at the Battle of Callinicum and recalled to the Empire's heart in Constantinople.

Justinian was without doubt clever but cruel. When part of Constantinople rose against him in the Nika riots of January, 532, he sent Belisarius and his fellow general Mundo to repress them in a savage massacre in the Hippodrome – witnessed by Procopius.

The following year Procopius accompanied Belisarius on his victorious expedition against the Vandal kingdom in North Africa and took part in the capture of Carthage. Procopius remained in Northern Africa with Belisarius' successor, Solomon the Eunuch, when Belisarius returned to Constantinople.

Procopius rejoined Belisarius for his campaign against the Ostrogothic kingdom in Italy and was there for the Gothic siege of Rome that lasted a year and nine days and ended in March, 538. He witnessed Belisarius' entry into the Gothic capital, Ravenna, in 540.

However at some point in the next few years Procopius seems to have been moved away from working with Belisarius. When the latter was sent back to Italy in 544 to cope with a further outbreak of the war with the Goths, Procopius appears to have no longer been with Belisarius' staff.

Procopius continued to record history and his works are both insightful and clear headed, distilling the complexities of the times into several classic books.

His death is thought to have been around 560.

Index of Contents
Book I
I
II
III
IV
V
VI

VII
VIII
IX
X
XI
XII
XIII
XIV
XV
XVI
XVII
XVIII
XIX
XX
XXI
XXII
XXIII
XXIV
XXV
XXVI
FOOTNOTES

Book II
I
II
III
IV
V
VI
VII
VIII
IX
X
XI
XII
XIII
XIV
XV
XVI
XVII
XVIII
XIX
XX
XXI
XXII
XXIII
XXIV
XXV
XXVI
XXVII
XXVIII

XXIX
XXX
FOOTNOTES

I

Procopius of Caesarea has written the history of the wars which Justinian, Emperor of the Romans, waged against the barbarians of the East and of the West, relating separately the events of each one, to the end that the long course of time may not overwhelm deeds of singular importance through lack of a record, and thus abandon them to oblivion and utterly obliterate them. The memory of these events he deemed would be a great thing and most helpful to men of the present time, and to future generations as well, in case time should ever again place men under a similar stress. For men who purpose to enter upon a war or are preparing themselves for any kind of struggle may derive some benefit from a narrative of a similar situation in history, inasmuch as this discloses the final result attained by men of an earlier day in a struggle of the same sort, and foreshadows, at least for those who are most prudent in planning, what outcome present events will probably have. Furthermore he had assurance that he was especially competent to write the history of these events, if for no other reason, because it fell to his lot, when appointed adviser to the general Belisarius, to be an eye-witness of practically all the events to be described. It was his conviction that while cleverness is appropriate to rhetoric, and inventiveness to poetry, truth alone is appropriate to history. In accordance with this principle he has not concealed the failures of even his most intimate acquaintances, but has written down with complete accuracy everything which befell those concerned, whether it happened to be done well or ill by them.

It will be evident that no more important or mightier deeds are to be found in history than those which have been enacted in these wars, provided one wishes to base his judgment on the truth. For in them more remarkable feats have been performed than in any other wars with which we are acquainted; unless, indeed, any reader of this narrative should give the place of honour to antiquity, and consider contemporary achievements unworthy to be counted remarkable. There are those, for example, who call the soldiers of the present day "bowmen," while to those of the most ancient times they wish to attribute such lofty terms as "hand-to-hand fighters," "shield-men," and other names of that sort; and they think that the valour of those times has by no means survived to the present, an opinion which is at once careless and wholly remote from actual experience of these matters. For the thought has never occurred to them that, as regards the Homeric bowmen who had the misfortune to be ridiculed by this term[1] derived from their art, they were neither carried by horse nor protected by spear or shield[2]. In fact there was no protection at all for their bodies; they entered battle on foot, and were compelled to conceal themselves, either singling out the shield of some comrade[3], or seeking safety behind a tombstone on a mound[4], from which position they could neither save themselves in case of rout, nor fall upon a flying foe. Least of all could they participate in a decisive struggle in the open, but they always seemed to be stealing something which belonged to the men who were engaged in the struggle. And apart from this they were so indifferent in their practice of archery that they drew the bowstring only to the breast[5], so that the missile sent forth was naturally impotent and harmless to those whom it hit[6]. Such, it is evident, was the archery of the past. But the bowmen of the present time go into battle wearing corselets and fitted out with greaves which extend up to the knee. From the right side hang their arrows, from the other the sword. And there are some who have a spear also attached to them and, at the shoulders, a sort of small shield without a grip, such as to cover the region of the face and neck. They are expert horsemen, and are able without difficulty to direct their bows to either side while riding at full speed, and to shoot an opponent whether in pursuit or in flight. They draw the bowstring along by the forehead about opposite the right ear, thereby charging the arrow with such an impetus as to kill whoever stands in the way, shield and corselet alike having no power to check its force. Still there are those who take into consideration none of these things, who reverence and worship the ancient times, and give no credit to modern improvements. But no such consideration will prevent the conclusion that most great and notable deeds have been performed in these wars. And the history of them will begin at some distance back, telling of the fortunes in war of the Romans and the Medes, their reverses and their successes.

II

[408 A.D.] When the Roman Emperor Arcadius was at the point of death in Byzantium, having a malechild, Theodosius, who was still unweaned, he felt grave fears not only for him but for the government as well, not knowing how he should provide wisely for both. For he perceived that, if he provided a partner in government for Theodosius, he would in fact be destroying his own son by bringing forward against him a foe clothed in the regal power; while if he set him alone over the empire, many would try to mount the throne, taking advantage, as they might be expected to do, of the helplessness of the child. These men would rise against the government, and, after destroying Theodosius, would make themselves tyrants without difficulty, since the boy had no kinsman in Byzantium to be his guardian. For Arcadius had no hope that the boy's uncle, Honorius, would succour him, inasmuch as the situation in Italy was already troublesome. And he was equally disturbed by the attitude of the Medes, fearing lest these barbarians should trample down the youthful emperor and do the Romans irreparable harm. When Arcadius was confronted with this difficult situation, though he had not shewn himself sagacious in other matters, he devised a plan which was destined to preserve without trouble both his child and his throne, either as a result of conversation with certain of the learned men, such as are usually found in numbers among the advisers of a sovereign, or from some divine inspiration which came to him. For in drawing up the writings of his will, he designated the child as his successor to the throne, but appointed as guardian over him Isdigerdes, the Persian King, enjoining upon him earnestly in his will to preserve the empire for Theodosius by all his power and foresight. So Arcadius died, having thus arranged his private affairs as well as those of the empire. But Isdigerdes, the Persian King, when he saw this writing which was duly delivered to him, being even before a sovereign whose nobility of character had won for him the greatest renown, did then display a virtue at once amazing and remarkable. For, loyally observing the behests of Arcadius, he adopted and continued without interruption a policy of profound peace with the Romans, and thus preserved the empire for Theodosius. Indeed, he straightway dispatched a letter to the Roman senate, not declining the office of guardian of the Emperor Theodosius, and threatening war against any who should attempt to enter into a conspiracy against him.

[441 A.D.] When Theodosius had grown to manhood and was in the prime of life, and Isdigerdes had been taken from the world by disease, Vararanes, the Persian King, invaded the Roman domains with a mighty army; however he did no damage, but returned to his home without accomplishing anything. This came about in the following way. Anatolius, General of the East, had, as it happened, been sent by the Emperor Theodosius as ambassador to the Persians, alone and unaccompanied; as he approached the Median army, solitary as he was, he leapt down from his horse, and advanced on foot toward Vararanes. And when Vararanes saw him, he enquired from those who were near who this man could be who was coming forward. And they replied that he was the general of the Romans. Thereupon the king was so dumbfounded by this excessive degree of respect that he himself wheeled his horse about and rode away, and the whole Persian host followed him. When he had reached his own territory, he received the envoy with great cordiality, and granted the treaty of peace on the terms which Anatolius desired of him; one condition, however, he added, that neither party should construct any new fortification in his own territory in the neighbourhood of the boundary line between the two countries. When this treaty had been executed, both sovereigns then continued to administer the affairs of their respective countries as seemed best to them.

III

At a later time the Persian King Perozes became involved in a war concerning boundaries with the nation of the Ephthalitae Huns, who are called White Huns, gathered an imposing army, and marched against them. The Ephthalitae are of the stock of the Huns in fact as well as in name; however they do not mingle with any of the Huns known to us, for they occupy a land neither adjoining nor even very near to them; but their territory lies immediately to the north of Persia; indeed their city, called Gorgo, is located over against the Persian frontier, and is consequently the centre of frequent contests concerning boundary lines between the two peoples. For they are not nomads like the other Hunnic peoples, but for a long period have been established in a goodly land. As a result of this they have never made any incursion into the Roman territory except in company with the Median army. They are the only ones among the Huns who have white bodies and countenances which are not ugly. It is also true that their manner of living is unlike that of their kinsmen, nor do they live a savage life as they do; but they are ruled by one king, and since they possess a lawful constitution, they observe right and justice in their dealings both with one another and with their neighbours, in no degree less than the Romans and the Persians. Moreover, the wealthy citizens are in the habit of attaching to themselves friends to the number of twenty or more, as the case may be, and these become permanently their banquet-companions, and have a share in all their property, enjoying some kind of a common right in this matter. Then, when the man who has gathered such a company together comes to die, it is the custom that all these men be borne alive into the tomb with him.

Perozes, marching against these Ephthalitae, was accompanied by an ambassador, Eusebius by name, who, as it happened, had been sent to his court by the Emperor Zeno. Now the Ephthalitae made it appear to their enemy that they had turned to flight because they were wholly terrified by their attack, and they retired with all speed to a place which was shut in on every side by precipitous mountains, and abundantly screened by a close forest of wide-spreading trees. Now as one advanced between the mountains to a great distance, a broad way appeared in the valley, extending apparently to an indefinite distance, but at the end it had no outlet at all, but terminated in the very midst of the circle of mountains. So Perozes, with no thought at all of treachery, and forgetting that he was marching in a hostile country, continued the pursuit without the least caution. A small body of the Huns were in flight before him, while the greater part of their force, by concealing themselves in the rough country, got in the rear of the hostile army; but as yet they desired not to be seen by them, in order that they might advance well into the trap and get as far as possible in among the mountains, and thus be no longer able to turn back. When the Medes began to realize all this (for they now began to have a glimmering of their peril), though they refrained from speaking of the situation themselves through fear of Perozes, yet they earnestly entreated Eusebius to urge upon the king, who was completely ignorant of his own plight, that he should take counsel rather than make an untimely display of daring, and consider well whether there was any way of safety open to them. So he went before Perozes, but by no means revealed the calamity which was upon them; instead he began with a fable, telling how a lion once happened upon a goat bound down and bleating on a mound of no very great height, and how the lion, bent upon making a feast of the goat, rushed forward with intent to seize him, but fell into a trench exceedingly deep, in which was a circular path, narrow and endless (for it had no outlet anywhere), which indeed the owners of the goat had constructed for this very purpose, and they had placed the goat above it to be a bait for the lion. When Perozes heard this, a fear came over him lest perchance the Medes had brought harm upon themselves by their pursuit of the enemy. He therefore advanced no further, but, remaining where he was, began to consider the situation. By this time the Huns were following him without any concealment, and were guarding the entrance of the place in order that their enemy might no longer be able to withdraw to the rear. Then at last the Persians saw clearly in what straits they were, and they felt that the situation was desperate; for they had no hope that they would ever escape from the peril. Then the king of the Ephthalitae sent some of his followers to Perozes; he upbraided him at length for his senseless foolhardiness, by which he had wantonly destroyed both himself and the Persian people, but he announced that even so the Huns would grant them deliverance, if Perozes should consent to prostrate himself before him as having proved himself master, and, taking the oaths traditional among the Persians, should give pledges that they would never again take the field against the nation of the Ephthalitae. When Perozes heard this, he held a consultation with the Magi who were present and enquired of them whether he must comply with the terms dictated by the enemy. The Magi replied that, as to the oath, he should settle the matter according to his own pleasure; as for the rest, however, he should circumvent his enemy by craft. And they reminded him that it was the custom among the Persians to prostrate themselves before the rising sun each day; he should, therefore, watch the time closely and meet the leader of the Ephthalitae at dawn, and then, turning toward the rising sun, make his obeisance. In this way, they explained, he would be able in the future to escape the ignominy of the deed. Perozes accordingly gave the pledges concerning the peace, and prostrated himself before his foe exactly as the Magi had suggested, and so, with the whole Median army intact, gladly retired homeward.

IV

Not long after this, disregarding the oath he had sworn, he was eager to avenge himself upon the Huns for the insult done him. He therefore straightway gathered together from the whole land all the Persians and their allies, and led them against the Ephthalitae; of all his sons he left behind him only one, Cabades by name, who, as it happened, was just past the age of boyhood; all the others, about thirty in number, he took with him. The Ephthalitae, upon learning of his invasion, were aggrieved at the deception they had suffered at the hands of their enemy, and bitterly reproached their king as having abandoned them to the Medes. He, with a laugh, enquired of them what in the world of theirs he had abandoned, whether their land or their arms or any other part of their possessions. They thereupon retorted that he had abandoned nothing, except, forsooth, the one opportunity on which, as it turned out, everything else depended. Now the Ephthalitae with all zeal demanded that they should go out to meet the invaders, but the king sought to restrain them at any rate for the moment. For he insisted that as yet they had received no definite information as to the invasion, for the Persians were still within their own boundaries. So, remaining where he was, he busied himself as follows. In the plain where the Persians were to make their irruption into the land of the Ephthalitae he marked off a tract of very great extent and made a deep trench of sufficient width; but in the centre he left a small portion of ground intact, enough to serve as a way for ten horses. Over the trench he placed reeds, and upon the reeds he scattered earth, thereby concealing the true surface. He then directed the forces of the Huns that, when the time came to retire inside the trench, they should draw themselves together into a narrow column and pass rather slowly across this neck of land, taking care that they should not fall into the ditch[7]. And he hung from the top of the royal banner the salt over which Perozes had once sworn the oath which he had disregarded in taking the field against the Huns. Now as long as he heard that the enemy were in their own territory, he remained at rest; but when he learned from his scouts that they had reached the city of Gorgo which lies on the extreme Persian frontier, and that departing thence they were now advancing against his army, remaining himself with the greater part of his troops inside the trench, he sent forward a small detachment with instructions to allow themselves to be seen at a distance by the enemy in the plain, and, when once they had been seen, to flee at full speed to the rear, keeping in mind his command concerning the trench as soon as they drew near to it. They did as directed, and, as they approached the trench, they drew themselves into a narrow column, and all passed over and joined the rest of the army. But the Persians, having no means of perceiving the stratagem, gave chase at full speed across a very level plain, possessed as they were by a spirit of fury against the enemy, and fell into the trench, every man of them, not alone the first but also those who followed in the rear. For since they entered into the pursuit with great fury, as I have said, they failed to notice the catastrophe which had befallen their leaders, but fell in on top of them with their horses and lances, so that, as was natural, they both destroyed them, and were themselves no less involved in ruin. Among them were Perozes and all his sons. And just as he was about to fall into this pit, they say that he realized the danger, and seized and threw from him the pearl which hung from his right ear, a gem of wonderful whiteness and greatly prized on account of its extraordinary size, in order, no doubt, that no one might wear it after him; for it was a thing exceedingly beautiful to look upon, such as no king before him had possessed. This story, however, seems to me untrustworthy, because a man who found himself in such peril would have thought of nothing else; but I suppose that his ear was crushed in this disaster, and the pearl disappeared somewhere or other. This pearl the Roman Emperor then made every effort to buy from the Ephthalitae, but was utterly unsuccessful. For the barbarians were not able to find it although they sought it with great labour. However, they say that the Ephthalitae found it later and sold it to Cabades.

The story of this pearl, as told by the Persians, is worth recounting, for perhaps to some it may not seem altogether incredible. For they say that it was lodged in its oyster in the sea which washes the Persian coast, and that the oyster was swimming not far from the shore; both its valves were standing open and the pearl lay between them, a wonderful sight and notable, for no pearl in all history could be compared with it at all, either in size or in beauty. A shark, then, of enormous size and dreadful fierceness, fell in love with this sight and followed close upon it, leaving it neither day nor night; even when he was compelled to take thought for food, he would only look about for something eatable where he was, and when he found some bit, he would snatch it up and eat it hurriedly; then overtaking the oyster immediately, he would sate himself again with the sight he loved. At length a fisherman, they say, noticed what was passing, but in terror of the monster he recoiled from the danger; however, he reported the whole matter to the king, Perozes. Now when Perozes heard his account, they say that a great longing for the pearl came over him, and he urged on this fisherman with many flatteries and hopes of reward. Unable to resist the importunities of the monarch, he is said to have addressed Perozes as follows: "My master, precious to a man is money, more precious still is his life, but most prized of all are his children; and being naturally constrained by his love for them a man might perhaps dare anything. Now I intend to make trial of the monster, and hope to make thee master of the pearl. And if I succeed in this struggle, it is plain that henceforth I shall be ranked among those who are counted blessed. For it is not unlikely that thou, as King of Kings, wilt reward me with all good things; and for me it will be sufficient, even if it so fall out that I gain no reward, to have shewn myself a benefactor of my master. But if it must needs be that I become the prey of this monster, thy task indeed it will be, O King, to requite my children for their father's death. Thus even after my death I shall still be a wage-earner among those closest to me, and thou wilt win greater fame for thy goodness, for in helping my children thou wilt confer a boon upon me, who shall have no power to thank thee for the benefit, because generosity is seen to be without alloy only when it is displayed towards the dead." With these words he departed. And when he came to the place where the oyster was accustomed to swim and the shark to follow, he seated himself there upon a rock, watching for an opportunity of catching the pearl alone without its admirer. As soon as it came about that the shark had happened upon something which would serve him for food, and was delaying over it, the fisherman left upon the beach those who were following him for this service, and made straight for the oyster with all his might; already he had seized it and was hastening with all speed to get out of the water, when the shark noticed him and rushed to the rescue. The fisherman saw him coming, and, when he was about to be overtaken not far from the beach, he hurled his booty with all his force upon the land, and was himself soon afterwards seized and destroyed. But the men who had been left upon the beach picked up the pearl, and, conveying it to the king, reported all that had happened. Such, then, is the story which the Persians relate, just as I have set it down, concerning this pearl. But I shall return to the previous narrative.

[484 A.D.] Thus Perozes was destroyed and the whole Persian army with him. For the few who by chance did not fall into the ditch found themselves at the mercy of the enemy. As a result of this experience a law was established among the Persians that, while marching in hostile territory, they should never engage in any pursuit, even if it should happen that the enemy had been driven back by force. Thereupon those who had not marched with Perozes and had remained in their own land chose as their king Cabades, the youngest son of Perozes, who was then the only one surviving. At that time, then, the Persians became subject and tributary to the Ephthalitae, until Cabades had established his power most securely and no longer deemed it necessary to pay the annual tribute to them. And the time these barbarians ruled over the Persians was two years.

V

But as time went on Cabades became more high-handed in the administration of the government, and introduced innovations into the constitution, among which was a law which he promulgated providing that Persians should have communal intercourse with their women, a measure which by no means pleased the common people. [486 A.D.] Accordingly they rose against him, removed him from the throne, and kept him in prison in chains. They then chose Blases, the brother of Perozes, to be their king, since, as has been said, no male offspring of Perozes was left, and it is not lawful among the Persians for any man by birth a common citizen to be set upon the throne, except in case the royal family be totally extinct. Blases, upon receiving the royal power, gathered together the nobles of the Persians and held a conference concerning Cabades; for it was not the wish of the majority to put the man to death. After the expression of many opinions on both sides there came forward a certain man of repute among the Persians, whose name was Gousanastades, and whose office that of "chanaranges" (which would be the Persian term for general); his official province lay on the very frontier of the Persian territory in a district which adjoins the land of the Ephthalitae. Holding up his knife, the kind with which the Persians were accustomed to trim their nails, of about the length of a man's finger, but not one-third as wide as a finger, he said: "You see this knife, how extremely small it is; nevertheless it is able at the present time to accomplish a deed, which, be assured, my dear Persians, a little later two myriads of mail-clad men could not bring to pass." This he said hinting that, if they did not put Cabades to death, he would straightway make trouble for the Persians. But they were altogether unwilling to put to death a man of the royal blood, and decided to confine him in a castle which it is their habit to call the "Prison of Oblivion." For if anyone is cast into it, the law permits no mention of him to be made thereafter, but death is the penalty for the man who speaks his name; for this reason it has received this title among the Persians. On one occasion, however, the History of the Armenians relates that the operation of the law regarding the Prison of Oblivion was suspended by the Persians in the following way.

There was once a truceless war, lasting two and thirty years, between the Persians and the Armenians, when Pacurius was king of the Persians, and of the Armenians, Arsaces, of the line of the Arsacidae. And by the long continuance of this war it came about that both sides suffered beyond measure, and especially the Armenians. But each nation was possessed by such great distrust of the other that neither of them could make overtures of peace to their opponents. In the meantime it happened that the Persians became engaged in a war with certain other barbarians who lived not far from the Armenians. Accordingly the Armenians, in their eagerness to make a display to the Persians of their goodwill and desire for peace, decided to invade the land of these barbarians, first revealing their plan to the Persians. Then they fell upon them unexpectedly and killed almost the whole population, old and young alike. Thereupon Pacurius, who was overjoyed at the deed, sent certain of his trusted friends to Arsaces, and giving him pledges of security, invited him to his presence. And when Arsaces came to him he shewed him every kindness, and treated him as a brother on an equal footing with himself. Then he bound him by the most solemn oaths, and he himself swore likewise, that in very truth the Persians and Armenians should thenceforth be friends and allies to each other; thereafter he straightway dismissed Arsaces to return to his own country.

Not long after this certain persons slandered Arsaces, saying that he was purposing to undertake some seditious enterprise. Pacurius was persuaded by these men and again summoned him, intimating that he was anxious to confer with him on general matters. And he, without any hesitation at all, came to the king, taking with him several of the most warlike among the Armenians, and among them Bassicius, who was at once his general and counsellor; for he was both brave and sagacious to a remarkable degree. Straightway, then, Pacurius heaped reproach and abuse upon both Arsaces and Bassicius, because, disregarding the sworn compact, they had so speedily turned their thoughts toward secession. They, however, denied the charge, and swore most insistently that no such thing had been considered by them. At first, therefore, Pacurius kept them under guard in disgrace, but after a time he enquired of the Magi what should be done with them. Now the Magi deemed it by no means just to condemn men who denied their guilt and had not been explicitly found guilty, but they suggested to him an artifice by which Arsaces himself might be compelled to become openly his own accuser. They bade him cover the floor of the royal tent with earth, one half from the land of Persia, and the other half from Armenia. This the king did as directed. Then the Magi, after putting the whole tent under a spell by means of some magic rites, bade the king take his walk there in company with Arsaces, reproaching him meanwhile with having violated the sworn agreement. They said, further, that they too must be present at the conversation, for in this way there would be witnesses of all that was said. Accordingly Pacurius straightway summoned Arsaces, and began to walk to and fro with him in the tent in the presence of the Magi; he enquired of the man why he had disregarded his sworn promises, and was setting about to harass the Persians and Armenians once more with grievous troubles. Now as long as the conversation took place on the ground which was covered with the earth from the land of Persia, Arsaces continued to make denial, and, pledging himself with the most fearful oaths, insisted that he was a faithful subject of Pacurius. But when, in the midst of his speaking, he came to the centre of the tent where they stepped upon Armenian earth, then, compelled by some unknown power, he suddenly changed the tone of his words to one of defiance, and from then on ceased not to threaten Pacurius and the Persians, announcing that he would have vengeance upon them for this insolence as soon as he should become his own master. These words of youthful folly he continued to utter as they walked all the way, until turning back, he came again to the earth from the Persian land. Thereupon, as if chanting a recantation, he was once more a suppliant, offering pitiable explanations to Pacurius. But when he came again to the Armenian earth, he returned to his threats. In this way he changed many times to one side and the other, and concealed none of his secrets. Then at length the Magi passed judgment against him as having violated the treaty and the oaths. Pacurius flayed Bassicius, and, making a bag of his skin, filled it with chaff and suspended it from a lofty tree. As for Arsaces, since Pacurius could by no means bring himself to kill a man of the royal blood, he confined him in the Prison of Oblivion.

After a time, when the Persians were marching against a barbarian nation, they were accompanied by an Armenian who had been especially intimate with Arsaces and had followed him when he went into the Persian land. This man proved himself a capable warrior in this campaign, as Pacurius observed, and was the chief cause of the Persian victory. For this reason Pacurius begged him to make any request he wished, assuring him that he would be refused nothing by him. The Armenian asked for nothing else than that he might for one day pay homage to Arsaces in the way he might desire. Now it annoyed the king exceedingly, that he should be compelled to set aside a law so ancient; however, in order to be wholly true to his word, he permitted that the request be granted. When the man found himself by the king's order in the Prison of Oblivion, he greeted Arsaces, and both men, embracing each other, joined their voices in a sweet lament, and, bewailing the hard fate that was upon them, were able only with difficulty to release each other from the embrace. Then, when they had sated themselves with weeping and ceased from tears, the Armenian bathed Arsaces, and completely adorned his person, neglecting nothing, and, putting on him the royal robe, caused him to recline on a bed of rushes. Then Arsaces entertained those present with a royal banquet just as was formerly his custom. During this feast many speeches were made over the cups which greatly pleased Arsaces, and many incidents occurred which delighted his heart. The drinking was prolonged until nightfall, all feeling the keenest delight in their mutual intercourse; at length they parted from each other with great reluctance, and separated thoroughly imbued with happiness. Then they tell how Arsaces said that after spending the sweetest day of his life, and enjoying the company of the man he had missed most of all, he would no longer willingly endure the miseries of life; and with these words, they say, he dispatched himself with a knife which, as it happened, he had purposely stolen at the banquet, and thus departed from among men. Such then is the story concerning this Arsaces, related in the Armenian History just as I have told it, and it was on that occasion that the law regarding the Prison of Oblivion was set aside. But I must return to the point from which I have strayed.

VI

While Cabades was in the prison he was cared for by his wife, who went in to him constantly and carried him supplies of food. Now the keeper of the prison began to make advances to her, for she was exceedingly beautiful to look upon. And when Cabades learned this from his wife, he bade her give herself over to the man to treat as he wished. In this way the keeper of the prison came to be familiar with the woman, and he conceived for her an extraordinary love, and as a result permitted her to go in to her husband just as she wished, and to depart from there again without interference from anyone. Now there was a Persian notable, Seoses by name, a devoted friend of Cabades, who was constantly in the neighbourhood of this prison, watching his opportunity, in the hope that he might in some way be able to effect his deliverance. And he sent word to Cabades through his wife that he was keeping horses and men in readiness not far from the prison, and he indicated to him a certain spot. Then one day as night drew near Cabades persuaded his wife to give him her own garment, and, dressing herself in his clothes, to sit instead of him in the prison where he usually sat. In this way, therefore, Cabades made his escape from the prison. For although the guards who were on duty saw him, they supposed that it was the woman, and therefore decided not to hinder or otherwise annoy him. At daybreak they saw in the cell the woman in her husband's clothes, and were so completely deceived as to think that Cabades was there, and this belief prevailed during several days, until Cabades had advanced well on his way. As to the fate which befell the woman after the stratagem had come to light, and the manner in which they punished her, I am unable to speak with accuracy. For the Persian accounts do not agree with each other, and for this reason I omit the narration of them.

Cabades, in company with Seoses, completely escaped detection, and reached the Ephthalitae Huns; there the king gave him his daughter in marriage, and then, since Cabades was now his son-in-law, he put under his command a very formidable army for a campaign against the Persians. This army the Persians were quite unwilling to encounter, and they made haste to flee in every direction. And when Cabades reached the territory where Gousanastades exercised his authority, he stated to some of his friends that he would appoint as chanaranges the first man of the Persians who should on that day come into his presence and offer his services. But even as he said this, he repented his speech, for there came to his mind a law of the Persians which ordains that offices among the

Persians shall not be conferred upon others than those to whom each particular honour belongs by right of birth. For he feared lest someone should come to him first who was not a kinsman of the present chanaranges, and that he would be compelled to set aside the law in order to keep his word. Even as he was considering this matter, chance brought it about that, without dishonouring the law, he could still keep his word. For the first man who came to him happened to be Adergoudounbades, a young man who was a relative of Gousanastades and an especially capable warrior. He addressed Cabades as "Lord," and was the first to do obeisance to him as king, and besought him to use him as a slave for any service whatever. [488 A.D.] So Cabades made his way into the royal palace without any trouble, and, taking Blases destitute of defenders, he put out his eyes, using the method of blinding commonly employed by the Persians against malefactors, that is, either by heating olive oil and pouring it, while boiling fiercely, into the wide-open eyes, or by heating in the fire an iron needle, and with this pricking the eyeballs. Thereafter Blases was kept in confinement, having ruled over the Persians two years. Gousanastades was put to death and Adergoudounbades was established in his place in the office of chanaranges, while Seoses was immediately proclaimed "adrastadaran salanes," a title designating the one set in authority over all magistrates and over the whole army. Seoses was the first and only man who held this office in Persia; for it was conferred on no one before or after that time. And the kingdom was strengthened by Cabades and guarded securely; for in shrewdness and activity he was surpassed by none.

VII

A little later Cabades was owing the king of the Ephthalitae a sum of money which he was not able to pay him, and he therefore requested the Roman emperor Anastasius to lend him this money. Whereupon Anastasius conferred with some of his friends and enquired of them whether this should be done; and they would not permit him to make the loan. For, as they pointed out, it was inexpedient to make more secure by means of their money the friendship between their enemies and the Ephthalitae; indeed it was better for the Romans to disturb their relations as much as possible. It was for this reason, and for no just cause, that Cabades decided to make an expedition against the Romans. [502 A.D.] First he invaded the land of the Armenians, moving with such rapidity as to anticipate the news of his coming, and, after plundering the greater part of it in a rapid campaign, he unexpectedly arrived at the city of Amida, which is situated in Mesopotamia, and, although the season was winter, he invested the town. Now the citizens of Amida had no soldiers at hand, seeing that it was a time of peace and prosperity, and in other respects were utterly unprepared; nevertheless they were quite unwilling to yield to the enemy, and shewed an unexpected fortitude in holding out against dangers and hardships.

Now there was among the Syrians a certain just man, Jacobus by name, who had trained himself with exactitude in matters pertaining to religion. This man had confined himself many years before in a place called Endielon, a day's journey from Amida, in order that he might with more security devote himself to pious contemplation. The men of this place, assisting his purpose, had surrounded him with a kind of fencing, in which the stakes were not continuous, but set at intervals, so that those who approached could see and hold converse with him. And they had constructed for him a small roof over his head, sufficient to keep off the rain and snow. There this man had been sitting for a long time, never yielding either to heat or cold, and sustaining his life with certain seeds, which he was accustomed to eat, not indeed every day, but only at long intervals. Now some of the Ephthalitae who were overrunning the country thereabout saw this Jacobus and with great eagerness drew their bows with intent to shoot at him. But the hands of every one of them became motionless and utterly unable to manage the bow. When this was noised about through the army and came to the ears of Cabades, he desired to see the thing with his own eyes; and when he saw it, both he and the Persians who were with him were seized with great astonishment, and he entreated

Jacobus to forgive the barbarians their crime. And he forgave them with a word, and the men were released from their distress. Cabades then bade the man ask for whatever he wished, supposing that he would ask for a great sum of money, and he also added with youthful recklessness that he would be refused nothing by him. But he requested Cabades to grant to him all the men who during that war should come to him as fugitives. This request Cabades granted, and gave him a written pledge of his personal safety. And great numbers of men, as might be expected, came flocking to him from all sides and found safety there; for the deed became widely known. Thus, then, did these things take place.

Cabades, in besieging Amida, brought against every part of the defences the engines known as rams; but the townspeople constantly broke off the heads of the rams by means of timbers thrown across them[8]. However, Cabades did not slacken his efforts until he realized that the wall could not be successfully assailed in this way. For, though he battered the wall many times, he was quite unable to break down any portion of the defence, or even to shake it; so secure had been the work of the builders who had constructed it long before. Failing in this, Cabades raised an artificial hill to threaten the city, considerably overtopping the wall; but the besieged, starting from the inside of their defences, made a tunnel extending under the hill, and from there stealthily carried out the earth, until they hollowed out a great part of the inside of the hill. However, the outside kept the form which it had at first assumed, and afforded no opportunity to anyone of discovering what was being done. Accordingly many Persians mounted it, thinking it safe, and stationed themselves on the summit with the purpose of shooting down upon the heads of those inside the fortifications. But with the great mass of men crowding upon it with a rush, the hill suddenly fell in and killed almost all of them. Cabades, then, finding no remedy for the situation, decided to raise the siege, and he issued orders to the army to retreat on the morrow. Then indeed the besieged, as though they had no thought of their danger, began laughingly from the fortifications to jeer at the barbarians. Besides this some courtesans shamelessly drew up their clothing and displayed to Cabades, who was standing close by, those parts of a woman's body which it is not proper that men should see uncovered. This was plainly seen by the Magi, and they thereupon came before the king and tried to prevent the retreat, declaring as their interpretation of what had happened that the citizens of Amida would shortly disclose to Cabades all their secret and hidden things. So the Persian army remained there.

Not many days later one of the Persians saw close by one of the towers the mouth of an old underground passage, which was insecurely concealed with some few small stones. In the night he came there alone, and, making trial of the entrance, got inside the circuit-wall; then at daybreak he reported the whole matter to Cabades. The king himself on the following night came to the spot with a few men, bringing ladders which he had made ready. And he was favoured by a piece of good fortune; for the defence of the very tower which happened to be nearest to the passage had fallen by lot to those of the Christians who are most careful in their observances, whom they call monks. These men, as chance would have it, were keeping some annual religious festival to God on that day. When night came on they all felt great weariness[9] on account of the festival, and, having sated themselves with food and drink beyond their wont, they fell into a sweet and gentle sleep, and were consequently quite unaware of what was going on. So the Persians made their way through the passage inside the fortifications, a few at a time, and, mounting the tower, they found the monks still sleeping and slew them to a man. When Cabades learned this, he brought his ladders up to the wall close by this tower. It was already day. And those of the townsmen who were keeping guard on the adjoining tower became aware of the disaster, and ran thither with all speed to give assistance. Then for a long time both sides struggled to crowd back the other, and already the townsmen were gaining the advantage, killing many of those who had mounted the wall, and throwing back the men on the ladders, and they came very near to averting the danger. But Cabades drew his sword and, terrifying the Persians constantly with it, rushed in person to the ladders and would not let them draw back, and death was the punishment for those who dared turn to leave. As a result of this the Persians by their numbers gained the upper hand and overcame their antagonists in the fight. So the city was captured by storm on the eightieth day after the beginning of the siege. [Jan. 11, 503 A.D.] There followed a great massacre of the townspeople, until one of the citizens, an old man and a priest, approached Cabades as he was riding into the city, and said that it was not a kingly act to slaughter captives. Then Cabades, still moved with passion, replied: "But why did you decide to fight against me?" And the old man answered quickly: "Because God willed to give Amida into thy hand not so much because of our decision as of thy valour." Cabades was pleased by this speech, and permitted no further slaughter, but he bade the Persians plunder the property and make slaves of the survivors, and he directed them to choose out for himself all the notables among them.

A short time after this he departed, leaving there to garrison the place a thousand men under command of Glones, a Persian, and some few unfortunates among the citizens of Amida who were destined to minister as servants to the daily wants of the Persians; he himself with all the remainder of the army and the captives marched away homeward. These captives were treated by Cabades with a generosity befitting a king; for after a short time he released all of them to return to their homes, but he pretended that they had escaped from him by stealth[10]; and the Roman Emperor, Anastasius, also shewed them honour worthy of their bravery, for he remitted to the city all the annual taxes for the space of seven years, and presented all of them as a body and each one of them separately with many good things, so that they came fully to forget the misfortunes which had befallen them. But this happened in later years.

VIII

At that time the Emperor Anastasius, upon learning that Amida was being besieged, dispatched with all speed an army of sufficient strength. But in this army there were general officers in command of every symmory[11], while the supreme command was divided between the following four generals: Areobindus, at that time General of the East, the son-in-law of Olyvrius, who had been Emperor in the West not long before; Celer, commander of the palace troops (this officer the Romans are accustomed to call "magister"); besides these still, there were the commanders of troops in Byzantium, Patricias, the Phrygian, and Hypatius, the nephew of the emperor; these four, then, were the generals. With them also was associated Justinus, who at a later time became emperor upon the death of Anastasius, and Patriciolus with his son Vitalianus, who raised an armed insurrection against the Emperor Anastasius not long afterwards and made himself tyrant; also Pharesmanes, a native of Colchis, and a man of exceptional ability as a warrior, and the Goths Godidisklus and Bessas, who were among those Goths who had not followed Theoderic when he went from Thrace into Italy, both of them men of the noblest birth and experienced in matters pertaining to warfare; many others, too, who were men of high station, joined this army. For such an army, they say, was never assembled by the Romans against the Persians either before or after that time. However, all these men did not assemble in one body, nor did they form a single army as they marched, but each commander by himself led his own division separately against the enemy. And as manager of the finances of the army Apion, an Aegyptian, was sent, a man of eminence among the patricians and extremely energetic; and the emperor in a written statement declared him partner in the royal power, in order that he might have authority to administer the finances as he wished.

Now this army was mustered with considerable delay, and advanced with little speed. As a result of this they did not find the barbarians in the Roman territory; for the Persians had made their attack suddenly, and had immediately withdrawn with all their booty to their own land. Now no one of the generals desired for the present to undertake the siege of the garrison left in Amida, for they learned that they had carried in a large supply of provisions; but they made haste to invade the land of the enemy. However they did not advance together against the barbarians but they encamped apart from one another as they proceeded. When Cabades learned this (for he happened to be close by), he came with all speed to the Roman frontier and confronted them. But the Romans had not yet learned that Cabades was moving against them with his whole force, and they supposed that some small Persian army was there. Accordingly the forces of Areobindus established their camp in a place called Arzamon, at a distance of two days' journey from the city of Constantina, and those of Patricius and Hypatius in a place called Siphrios, which is distant not less than three hundred and fifty stades from the city of Amida. As for Celer, he had not yet arrived.

Areobindus, when he ascertained that Cabades was coming upon them with his whole army, abandoned his camp, and, in company with all his men, turned to flight and retired on the run to Constantina. And the enemy, coming up not long afterwards, captured the camp without a man in it and all the money it contained. From there they advanced swiftly against the other Roman army. Now the troops of Patricius and Hypatius had happened upon eight hundred Ephthalitae who were marching in advance of the Persian army, and they had killed practically all of them. Then, since they had learned nothing of Cabades and the Persian army, supposing that they had won the victory, they began to conduct themselves with less caution. At any rate they had stacked their arms and were preparing themselves a lunch; for already the appropriate time of day was drawing near. Now a small stream flowed in this place and in it the Romans began to wash the pieces of meat which they were about to eat; some, too, distressed by the heat, were bathing themselves in the stream; and in consequence the brook flowed on with a muddy current. But while Cabades, learning what had befallen the Ephthalitae, was advancing against the enemy with all speed, he noticed that the water of the brook was disturbed, and divining what was going on, he came to the conclusion that his opponents were unprepared, and gave orders to charge upon them immediately at full speed. [Aug., 503 A.D.] Straightway, then, they fell upon them feasting and unarmed. And the Romans did not withstand their onset, nor did they once think of resistance, but they began to flee as each one could; and some of them were captured and slain, while others climbed the hill which rises there and threw themselves down the cliff in panic and much confusion. And they say that not a man escaped from there; but Patricius and Hypatius had succeeded in getting away at the beginning of the onset. After this Cabades retired homeward with his whole army, since hostile Huns had made an invasion into his land, and with this people he waged a long war in the northerly portion of his realm. In the meantime the other Roman army also came, but they did nothing worth recounting, because, it seems, no one was made commander-in-chief of the expedition; but all the generals were of equal rank, and consequently they were always opposing one another's opinions and were utterly unable to unite. However Celer, with his contingent, crossed the Nymphius River and made some sort of an invasion into Arzanene. This river is one very close to Martyropolis, about three hundred stades from Amida. So Celer's troops plundered the country thereabout and returned not long after, and the whole invasion was completed in a short time.

IX

After this Areobindus went to Byzantium at the summons of the emperor, while the other generals reached Amida, and, in spite of the winter season, invested it. And although they made many attempts they were unable to carry the fortress by storm, but they were on the point of accomplishing their object by starvation; for all the provisions of the besieged were exhausted. The generals, however, had ascertained nothing of the straits in which the enemy were; but since they saw that their own troops were distressed by the labour of the siege and the wintry weather, and at the same time suspected that a Persian army would be coming upon them before long, they were eager to quit the place on any terms whatever. The Persians, on their part, not knowing what would become of them in such terrible straits, continued to conceal scrupulously their lack of the necessities of life, and made it appear that they had an abundance of all provisions, wishing to return to their homes with the reputation of honour. So a proposal was discussed between them, according to which the Persians were to deliver over the city to the Romans upon receipt of one thousand pounds of gold. Both parties then gladly executed the terms of the agreement, and the son of Glones, upon receiving the money, delivered over Amida to the Romans. For Glones himself had already died in the following manner.

When the Romans had not yet encamped before the city of Amida but were not far from its vicinity, a certain countryman, who was accustomed to enter the city secretly with fowls and loaves and many other delicacies, which he sold to this Glones at a great price, came before the general Patricius and promised to deliver into his hands Glones and two hundred Persians, if he should receive from him assurance of some requital. And the general promised that he should have everything he desired, and thus dismissed the fellow. He then tore his garments in a dreadful manner, and, assuming the aspect of one who had been weeping, entered the city. And coming before Glones, and tearing his hair he said: "O Master, I happened to be bringing in for you all the good things from my village, when some Roman soldiers chanced upon me (for, as you know, they are constantly wandering about the country here in small bands and doing violence to the miserable country-folk), and they inflicted upon me blows not to be endured, and, taking away everything, they departed, the robbers, whose ancient custom it is to fear the Persians and to beat the farmers. But do you, O Master, take thought to defend yourself and us and the Persians. For if you go hunting into the outskirts of the city, you will find rare game. For the accursed rascals go about by fours or fives to do their robbery." Thus he spoke. And Glones was persuaded, and enquired of the fellow about how many Persians he thought would be sufficient for him to carry out the enterprise. He said that about fifty would do, for they would never meet more than five of them going together; however, in order to forestall any unexpected circumstance, it would do no harm to take with him even one hundred men; and if he should double this number it would be still better from every point of view; for no harm could come to a man from the larger number. Glones accordingly picked out two hundred horsemen and bade the fellow lead the way for them. But he insisted that it was better for him to be sent first to spy out the ground, and, if he should bring back word that he had seen Romans still going about in the same districts, that then the Persians should make their sally at the fitting moment. Accordingly, since he seemed to Glones to speak well, he was sent forward by his own order. Then he came before the general Patricius and explained everything; and the general sent with him two of his own body-guard and a thousand soldiers. These he concealed about a village called Thilasamon, forty stades distant from Amida, among valleys and woody places, and instructed them to remain there in this ambush; he himself then proceeded to the city on the run, and telling Glones that the prey was ready, he led him and the two hundred horsemen upon the ambush of the enemy. And when they passed the spot where the Romans were lying in wait, without being observed by Glones or any of the Persians, he roused the Romans from their ambuscade and pointed out to them the enemy. And when the Persians saw the men coming against them, they were astounded at the suddenness of the thing, and were in much distress what to do. For neither could they retire to the rear, since their opponents were behind them, nor were they able to flee anywhere else in a hostile land. But as well as they could under the circumstances, they arrayed themselves for battle and tried to drive back their assailants; but being at a great disadvantage in numbers they were vanquished, and all of them together with Glones were destroyed. Now when the son of Glones learned of this, being deeply grieved and at the same time furious with anger because he had not been able to defend his father, he fired the sanctuary of Symeon, a holy man, where Glones had his lodging. It must be said, however, that with the exception of this one building, neither Glones nor Cabades, nor indeed any other of the Persians, saw fit either to tear down or to destroy in any other way any building in Amida at any rate, or outside this city. But I shall return to the previous narrative.

[504 A.D.] Thus the Romans by giving the money recovered Amida two years after it had been captured by the enemy. And when they got into the city, their own negligence and the hardships under which the Persians had maintained themselves were discovered. For upon reckoning the amount of grain left there and the number of barbarians who had gone out, they found that rations for about seven days were left in the city, although Glones and his son had been for a long time doling out provisions to the Persians more sparingly than they were needed. For to the Romans who had remained with them in the city, as I have stated above, they had decided to dispense nothing at all from the time when their enemy began the siege; and so these men at first resorted to unaccustomed foods and laid hold on every forbidden thing, and at the last they even tasted each other's blood. So the generals realized that they had been deceived by the barbarians, and they reproached the soldiers for their lack of self-control, because they had shewn themselves wanting in obedience to them, when it was possible to capture as prisoners of war such a multitude of Persians and the son of Glones and the city itself, while they had in consequence attached to themselves signal disgrace by carrying Roman money to the enemy, and had taken Amida from the Persians by purchasing it with silver. [506 A.D.] After this the Persians, since their war with the Huns kept dragging on, entered into a treaty with the Romans, which was arranged by them for seven years, and was made by the Roman Celer and the Persian Aspebedes; both armies then retired homeward and remained at peace. Thus, then, as has been told, began the war of the Romans and the Persians, and to this end did it come. But I shall now turn to the narration of the events touching the Caspian Gates.

X

The Taurus mountain range of Cilicia passes first Cappadocia and Armenia and the land of the so-called Persarmenians, then also Albania and Iberia and all the other countries in this region, both independent and subject to Persia. For it extends to a great distance, and as one proceeds along this range, it always spreads out to an extraordinary breadth and rises to an imposing height. And as one passes beyond the boundary of Iberia there is a sort of path in a very narrow passage, extending for a distance of fifty stades. This path terminates in a place cut off by cliffs and, as it seems, absolutely impossible to pass through. For from there no way out appears, except indeed a small gate set there by nature, just as if it had been made by the hand of man, which has been called from of old the Caspian Gates. From there on there are plains suitable for riding and extremely well watered, and extensive tracts used as pasture land for horses, and level besides. Here almost all the nations of the Huns are settled, extending as far as the Maeotic lake. Now if these Huns go through the gate which I have just mentioned into the land of the Persians and the Romans, they come with their horses fresh and without making any detour or encountering any precipitous places, except in those fifty stades over which, as has been said, they pass to the boundary of Iberia. If, however, they go by any other passes, they reach their destination with great difficulty, and can no longer use the same horses. For the detours which they are forced to make are many and steep besides. When this was observed by Alexander, the son of Philip, he constructed gates in the aforesaid place and established a fortress there. And this was held by many men in turn as time went on, and finally by Ambazouces, a Hun by birth, but a friend of the Romans and the Emperor Anastasius. Now when this Ambazouces had reached an advanced age and was near to death, he sent to Anastasius asking that money be given him, on condition that he hand over the fortress and the Caspian Gates to the Romans. But the Emperor Anastasius was incapable of doing anything without careful investigation, nor was it his custom to act thus: reasoning, therefore, that it was impossible for him to support soldiers in a place which was destitute of all good things, and which had nowhere in the neighbourhood a nation subject to the Romans, he expressed deep gratitude to the man for his good-will toward him, but by no means accepted this proposition. So Ambazouces died of disease not long afterwards, and Cabades overpowered his sons and took possession of the Gates.

The Emperor Anastasius, after concluding the treaty with Cabades, built a city in a place called Daras, exceedingly strong and of real importance, bearing the name of the emperor himself. Now this place is distant from the city of Nisibis one hundred stades lacking two, and from the boundary line which divides the Romans from the Persians about twenty-eight. And the Persians, though eager to prevent the building, were quite unable to do so, being constrained by the war with the Huns in which they were engaged. But as soon as Cabades brought this to an end, he sent to the Romans and accused them of having built a city hard by the Persian frontier, though this had been forbidden in the agreement previously made between the Medes and the Romans[12]. At that time, therefore, the Emperor Anastasius desired, partly by threats, and partly by emphasizing his friendship with him and by bribing him with no mean sum of money, to deceive him and to remove the accusation. And another city also was built by this emperor, similar to the first, in Armenia, hard by the boundaries of Persarmenia; now in this place there had been a village from of old, but it had taken on the dignity of a city by the favour of the Emperor Theodosius even to the name, for it had come to be named after him[13]. But Anastasius surrounded it with a very substantial wall, and thus gave offence to the Persians no less than by the other city; for both of them are strongholds menacing their country.

XI

[Aug. 1, 518 A.D.] And when a little later Anastasius died, Justinus received the empire, forcing aside all the kinsmen of Anastasius, although they were numerous and also very distinguished. Then indeed a sort of anxiety came over Cabades, lest the Persians should make some attempt to overthrow his house as soon as he should end his life; for it was certain that he would not pass on the kingdom to any one of his sons without opposition. For while the law called to the throne the eldest of his children Caoses by reason of his age, he was by no means pleasing to Cabades; and the father's judgment did violence to the law of nature and of custom as well. And Zames, who was second in age, having had one of his eyes struck out, was prevented by the law. For it is not lawful for a one-eyed man or one having any other deformity to become king over the Persians. But Chosroes, who was born to him by the sister of Aspebedes, the father loved exceedingly; seeing, however, that all the Persians, practically speaking, felt an extravagant admiration for the manliness of Zames (for he was a capable warrior), and worshipped his other virtues, he feared lest they should rise against Chosroes and do irreparable harm to the family and to the kingdom. Therefore it seemed best to him to arrange with the Romans to put an end both to the war and the causes of war, on condition that Chosroes be made an adopted son of the Emperor Justinus; for only in this way could he preserve stability in the government. Accordingly he sent envoys to treat of this matter and a letter to the Emperor Justinus in Byzantium. And the letter was written in this wise: "Unjust indeed has been the treatment which we have received at the hands of the Romans, as even you yourself know, but I have seen fit to abandon entirely all the charges against you, being assured of this, that the most truly victorious of all men would be those who, with justice on their side, are still willingly overcome and vanquished by their friends. However I ask of you a certain favour in return for this, which would bind together in kinship and in the good-will which would naturally spring from this relation not only ourselves but also all our subjects, and which would be calculated to bring us to a satiety of the blessings of peace. My proposal, then, is this, that you should make my son Chosroes, who will be my successor to the throne, your adopted son."

When this message was brought to the Emperor Justinus, he himself was overjoyed and Justinian also, the nephew of the emperor, who indeed was expected to receive from him the empire. And they were making all haste to perform the act of setting down in Writing the adoption, as the law of the Romans prescribes, and would have done so, had they not been prevented by Proclus, who was at that time a counsellor to the emperor, holding the office of quaestor, as it is called, a just man and one whom it was manifestly impossible to bribe; for this reason he neither readily proposed any law, nor was he willing to disturb in any way the settled order of things; and he at that time also opposed the proposition, speaking as follows: "To venture on novel projects is not my custom, and indeed I dread them more than any others; for where there is innovation security is by no means preserved. And it seems to me that, even if one should be especially bold in this matter, he would feel reluctance to do the thing and would tremble at the storm which would arise from it; for I believe that nothing else is before our consideration at the present time than the question how we may hand over the Roman empire to the Persians on a seemly pretext. For they make no concealment nor do they employ any blinds, but explicitly acknowledging their purpose they claim without more ado to rob us of our empire, seeking to veil the manifestness of their deceit under a shew of simplicity, and hide a shameless intent behind a pretended unconcern. And yet both of you ought to repel this attempt of the barbarians with all your power; thou, O Emperor, in order that thou mayst not be the last Emperor of the Romans, and thou, O General, that thou mayst not prove a stumbling block to thyself as regards coming to the throne. For other crafty devices which are commonly concealed by a pretentious shew of words might perhaps need an interpreter for the many, but this embassy openly and straight from the very first words means to make this Chosroes, whoever he is, the adopted heir of the Roman Emperor. For I would have you reason thus in this matter: by nature the possessions of fathers are due to their sons and while the laws among all men are always in conflict with each other by reason of their varying nature, in this matter both among the Romans and among all barbarians they are in agreement and harmony with each other, in that they declare sons to be masters of their fathers' inheritance. Take this first resolve if you choose: if you do you must agree to all its consequences."

Thus spoke Proclus; and the emperor and his nephew gave ear to his words and deliberated upon what should be done. In the meantime Cabades sent another letter also to the Emperor Justinus, asking him to send men of repute in order to establish peace with him, and to indicate by letter the manner in which it would be his desire to accomplish the adoption of his son. And then, indeed, still more than before Proclus decried the attempt of the Persians, and insisted that their concern was to make over to themselves as securely as possible the Roman power. And he proposed as his opinion that the peace should be concluded with them with all possible speed, and that the noblest men should be sent by the emperor for this purpose; and that these men must answer plainly to Cabades, when he enquired in what manner the adoption of Chosroes should be accomplished, that it must be of the sort befitting a barbarian, and his meaning was that the barbarians adopt sons, not by a document, but by arms and armour[14]. Accordingly the Emperor Justinus dismissed the envoys, promising that men who were the noblest of the Romans would follow them not long afterwards, and that they would arrange a settlement regarding the peace and regarding Chosroes in the best possible way. He also answered Cabades by letter to the same effect. Accordingly there were sent from the Romans Hypatius, the nephew of Anastasius, the late emperor, a patrician who also held the office of General of the East, and Rufinus, the son of Silvanus, a man of note among the patricians and known to Cabades through their fathers; from the Persians came one of great power and high authority, Seoses by name, whose title was adrastadaran salanes, and Mebodes, who held the office of magister. These men came together at a certain spot which is on the boundary line between the land of the Romans and the Persians: there they met and negotiated as to how they should do away with their differences and settle effectually the question of the peace. Chosroes also came to the Tigris River, which is distant from the city of Nisibis about two days journey, in order that, when the details of the peace should seem to both parties to be as well arranged as possible, he might betake himself in person to Byzantium. Now many words were spoken on both sides touching the differences between them, and in particular Seoses made mention of the land of Colchis, which is now called Lazica, saying that it had been subject to the Persians from of old and that the Romans had taken it from them by violence and held it on no just grounds. When the Romans heard this, they were indignant to think that even Lazica should be disputed by the Persians.

And when they in turn stated that the adoption of Chosroes must take place just as is proper for a barbarian, it seemed to the Persians unbearable. The two parties therefore separated and departed homeward, and Chosroes with nothing accomplished was off to his father, deeply injured at what had taken place and vowing vengeance on the Romans for their insult to him.

After this Mebodes began to slander Seoses to Cabades, saying that he had proposed the discussion of Lazica purposely, although he had not been instructed to do so by his master, thereby frustrating the peace, and also that he had had words previously with Hypatius, who was by no means well-disposed toward his own sovereign and was trying to prevent the conclusion of peace and the adoption of Chosroes; and many other accusations also were brought forward by the enemies of Seoses, and he was summoned to trial. Now the whole Persian council gathered to sit in judgment moved more by envy than by respect for the law. For they were thoroughly hostile to his office, which was unfamiliar to them, and also were embittered by the natural temper of the man. For while Seoses was a man quite impossible to bribe, and a most exact respecter of justice, he was afflicted with a degree of arrogance not to be compared with that of any other. This quality, indeed, seems to be inbred in the Persian officials, but in Seoses even they thought that the malady had developed to an altogether extraordinary degree. So his accusers said all those things which have been indicated above, and added to this that the man was by no means willing to live in the established fashion or to uphold the institutions of the Persians. For he both reverenced strange divinities, and lately, when his wife had died, he had buried her, though it was forbidden by the laws of the Persians ever to hide in the earth the bodies of the dead. The judges therefore condemned the man to death, while Cabades, though seeming to be deeply moved with sympathy as a friend of Seoses, was by no means willing to rescue him. He did not, on the other hand, make it known that he was angry with him, but, as he said, he was not willing to undo the laws of the Persians, although he owed the man the price of his life, since Seoses was chiefly responsible both for the fact that he was alive and also that he was king. Thus, then, Seoses was condemned and was removed from among men. And the office which began with him ended also with him. For no other man has been made adrastadaran salanes. Rufinus also slandered Hypatius to the emperor. As a result of this the emperor reduced him from his office, and tortured most cruelly certain of his associates only to find out that this slander was absolutely unsound; beyond this, however, he did Hypatius no harm.

XII

Immediately after this, Cabades, though eager to make some kind of an invasion into the land of the Romans, was utterly unable to do so on account of the following obstacle which happened to arise. The Iberians, who live in Asia, are settled in the immediate neighbourhood of the Caspian Gates, which lie to the north of them. Adjoining them on the left towards the west is Lazica, and on the right towards the east are the Persian peoples. This nation is Christian and they guard the rites of this faith more closely than any other men known to us, but they have been subjects of the Persian king, as it happens, from ancient times. And just then Cabades was desirous of forcing them to adopt the rites of his own religion. And he enjoined upon their king, Gourgenes, to do all things as the Persians are accustomed to do them, and in particular not under any circumstances to hide their dead in the earth, but to throw them all to the birds and dogs. For this reason, then, Gourgenes wished to go over to the Emperor Justinus, and he asked that he might receive pledges that the Romans would never abandon the Iberians to the Persians. And the emperor gave him these pledges with great eagerness, and he sent Probus, the nephew of the late emperor Anastasius, a man of patrician rank, with a great sum of money to Bosporus, that he might win over with money an army of Huns and send them as allies to the Iberians. This Bosporus is a city by the sea, on the left as one sails into the so-called Euxine Sea, twenty days journey distant from the city of Cherson, which is the limit of the Roman territory. Between these cities everything is held by the Huns. Now in ancient times the people of Bosporus were autonomous, but lately they had decided to become subject to the Emperor Justinus. Probus, however, departed from there without accomplishing his mission, and the emperor sent Peter as general with some Huns to Lazica to fight with all their strength for Gourgenes. Meanwhile Cabades sent a very considerable army against Gourgenes and the Iberians, and as general a Persian bearing the title of "varizes," Boes by name. Then it was seen that Gourgenes was too weak to withstand the attack of the Persians, for the help from the Romans was insufficient, and with all the notables of the Iberians he fled to Lazica, taking with him his wife and children and also his brothers, of whom Peranius was the eldest. And when they had reached the boundaries of Lazica, they remained there, and, sheltering themselves by the roughness of the country, they took their stand against the enemy. And the Persians followed after them but did nothing deserving even of mention since the circumstance of the rough country was against them.

Thereafter the Iberians presented themselves at Byzantium and Petrus came to the emperor at his summons; and from then on the emperor demanded that he should assist the Lazi to guard their country, even against their will, and he sent an army and Eirenaeus in command of it. Now there are two fortresses in Lazica[15] which one comes upon immediately upon entering their country from the boundaries of Iberia, and the defence of them had been from of old in charge of the natives, although they experienced great hardship in this matter; for neither corn nor wine nor any other good thing is produced there. Nor indeed can anything be carried in from elsewhere on account of the narrowness of the paths, unless it be carried by men. However, the Lazi were able to live on a certain kind of millet which grows there, since they were accustomed to it. These garrisons the emperor removed from the place and commanded that Roman soldiers should be stationed there to guard the fortresses. And at first the Lazi with difficulty brought in provisions for these soldiers, but later they gave up the service and the Romans abandoned these forts, whereupon the Persians with no trouble took possession of them. This then happened in Lazica.

And the Romans, under the leadership of Sittas and Belisarius, made an inroad into Persarmenia, a territory subject to the Persians, where they plundered a large tract of country and then withdrew with a great multitude of Armenian captives. These two men were both youths and wearing their first beards[16], body-guards of the general Justinian, who later shared the empire with his uncle Justinus. But when a second inroad had been made by the Romans into Armenia, Narses and Aratius unexpectedly confronted them and engaged them in battle. These men not long after this came to the Romans as deserters, and made the expedition to Italy with Belisarius; but on the present occasion they joined battle with the forces of Sittas and Belisarius and gained the advantage over them. An invasion was also made near the city of Nisibis by another Roman army under command of Libelarius of Thrace. This army retired abruptly in flight although no one came out against thorn. And because of this the emperor reduced Libelarius from his office and appointed Belisarius commander of the troops in Daras. It was at that time that Procopius, who wrote this history, was chosen as his adviser. [527 A.D.]

XIII

[Apr. 1, 527] Not long after this Justinus, who had declared his nephew Justinian emperor with him, died, and thus the empire came to Justinian alone. [Aug. 1, 527] This Justinian commanded Belisarius to build a fortress in a place called Mindouos, which is over against the very boundary of Persia, on the left as one goes to Nisibis. He accordingly with great haste began to carry out the decision of the emperor, and the fort was already rising to a considerable height by reason of the great number of artisans. But the Persians forbade them to build any further, threatening that, not with words alone but also with deeds, they would at no distant time obstruct the work. When the emperor heard this, inasmuch as Belisarius was not able to beat off the Persians from the place with the army he had, he ordered another army to go thither, and also Coutzes and Bouzes, who at that time commanded the soldiers in Libanus[17]. These two were brothers from Thrace, both young and inclined to be rash in engaging with the enemy. So both armies were gathered together and came in full force to the scene of the building operations, the Persians in order to hinder the work with all their power, and the Romans to defend the labourers. And a fierce battle took place in which the Romans were defeated, and there was a great slaughter of them, while some also were made captive by the enemy. Among these was Coutzes himself. All these captives the Persians led away to their own country, and, putting them in chains, confined them permanently in a cave; as for the fort, since no one defended it any longer, they razed what had been built to the ground.

After this the Emperor Justinian appointed Belisarius General of the East and bade him make an expedition against the Persians. And he collected a very formidable army and came to Daras. Hermogenes also came to him from the emperor to assist in setting the army in order, holding the office of magister; this man was formerly counsellor to Vitalianus at the time when he was at war with the Emperor Anastasius. The emperor also sent Rufinus as ambassador, commanding him to remain in Hierapolis on the Euphrates River until he himself should give the word. For already much was being said on both sides concerning peace. Suddenly, however, someone reported to Belisarius and Hermogenes that the Persians were expected to invade the land of the Romans, being eager to capture the city of Daras. And when they heard this, they prepared for the battle as follows. [July, 530] Not far from the gate which lies opposite the city of Nisibis, about a stone's throw away, they dug a deep trench with many passages across it. Now this trench was not dug in a straight line, but in the following manner. In the middle there was a rather short portion straight, and at either end of this there were dug two cross trenches at right angles to the first; and starting from the extremities of the two cross trenches, they continued two straight trenches in the original direction to a very great distance. Not long afterwards the Persians came with a great army, and all of them made camp in a place called Ammodios, at a distance of twenty stades from the city of Daras. Among the leaders of this army were Pityaxes and the one-eyed Baresmanas. But one general held command over them all, a Persian, whose title was "mirranes" (for thus the Persians designate this office), Perozes by name. This Perozes immediately sent to Belisarius bidding him make ready the bath: for he wished to bathe there on the following day. Accordingly the Romans made the most vigorous preparations for the encounter, with the expectation that they would fight on the succeeding day.

At sunrise, seeing the enemy advancing against them, they arrayed themselves as follows[18]. The extremity of the left straight trench which joined the cross trench, as far as the hill which rises here, was held by Bouzes with a large force of horsemen and by Pharas the Erulian with three hundred of his nation. On the right of these, outside the trench, at the angle formed by the cross trench and the straight section which extended from that point, were Sunicas and Aigan, Massagetae by birth, with six hundred horsemen, in order that, if those under Bouzes and Pharas should be driven back, they might, by moving quickly on the flank, and getting in the rear of the enemy, be able easily to support the Romans at that point. On the other wing also they were arrayed in the same manner; for the extremity of the straight trench was held by a large force of horsemen, who were commanded by John, son of Nicetas, and by Cyril and Marcellus; with them also were Germanus and Dorotheus; while at the angle on the right six hundred horsemen took their stand, commanded by Simmas and Ascan, Massagetae, in order that, as has been said, in case the forces of John should by any chance be driven back, they might move out from there and attack the rear of the Persians. Thus all along the trench stood the detachments of cavalry and the infantry. And behind these in the middle stood the forces of Belisarius and Hermogenes. Thus the Romans arrayed themselves, amounting to five-and-twenty thousand; but the Persian army consisted of forty thousand horse and foot, and they all stood close together facing the front, so as to make the front of the phalanx as deep as possible. Then for a long time neither side began battle with the other, but the Persians seemed to be wondering at the good order of the Romans, and appeared at a loss what to do under the circumstances.

In the late afternoon a certain detachment of the horsemen who held the right wing, separating themselves from the rest of the army, came against the forces of Bouzes and Pharas. And the Romans retired a short distance to the rear. The Persians, however, did not pursue them, but remained there, fearing, I suppose, some move to surround them on the part of the enemy. Then the Romans who had turned to flight suddenly rushed upon them. And the Persians did not withstand their onset and rode back to the phalanx, and again the forces of Bouzes and Pharas stationed themselves in their own position. In this skirmish seven of the Persians fell, and the Romans gained possession of their bodies; thereafter both armies remained quietly in position. But one Persian, a young man, riding up very close to the Roman army, began to challenge all of them, calling for whoever wished to do battle with him. And no one of the whole army dared face the danger, except a certain Andreas, one of the personal attendants of Bouzes, not a soldier nor one who had ever practised at all the business of war, but a trainer of youths in charge of a certain wrestling school in Byzantium. Through this it came about that he was following the army, for he cared for the person of Bouzes in the bath; his birthplace was Byzantium. This man alone had the courage, without being ordered by Bouzes or anyone else, to go out of his own accord to meet the man in single combat. And he caught the barbarian while still considering how he should deliver his attack, and hit him with his spear on the right breast. And the Persian did not bear the blow delivered by a man of such exceptional strength, and fell from his horse to the earth. Then Andreas with a small knife slew him like a sacrificial animal as he lay on his back, and a mighty shout was raised both from the city wall and from the Roman army. But the Persians were deeply vexed at the outcome and sent forth another horseman for the same purpose, a manly fellow and well favoured as to bodily size, but not a youth, for some of the hair on his head already shewed grey. This horseman came up along the hostile army, and, brandishing vehemently the whip with which he was accustomed to strike his horse, he summoned to battle whoever among the Romans was willing. And when no one went out against him, Andreas, without attracting the notice of anyone, once more came forth, although he had been forbidden to do so by Hermogenes. So both rushed madly upon each other with their spears, and the weapons, driven against their corselets, were turned aside with mighty force, and the horses, striking together their heads, fell themselves and threw off their riders. And both the two men, falling very close to each other, made great haste to rise to their feet, but the Persian was not able to do this easily because his size was against him, while Andreas, anticipating him (for his practice in the wrestling school gave him this advantage), smote him as he was rising on his knee, and as he fell again to the ground dispatched him. Then a roar went up from the wall and from the Roman army as great, if not greater, than before; and the Persians broke their phalanx and withdrew to Ammodios, while the Romans, raising the pæan, went inside the fortifications; for already it was growing dark. Thus both armies passed that night.

XIV

On the following day ten thousand soldiers arrived who had been summoned by the Persians from the city of Nisibis, and Belisarius and Hermogenes wrote to the mirranes as follows: "The first blessing is peace, as is agreed by all men who have even a small share of reason. It follows that if anyone should be a destroyer of it, he would be most responsible not only to those near him but also to his whole nation for the troubles which come. The best general, therefore, is that one who is able to bring about peace from war. But you, when affairs were well settled between the Romans and the Persians, have seen fit to bring upon us a war without cause, although the counsels of each king are looking toward peace, and although our envoys are already present in the neighbourhood, who will at no distant time settle all the points of dispute in talking over the situation together, unless some irreparable harm coming from your invasion proves sufficient to frustrate for us this hope. But lead away as soon as possible your army to the land of the Persians, and do not stand in the way of the greatest blessings, lest at some time you be held responsible by the Persians, as is probable, for the disasters which will come to pass." When the mirranes saw this letter brought to him, he replied as follows: "I should have been persuaded by what you write, and should have done what you demand, were the letter not, as it happens, from Romans, for whom the making of promises is easy, but the fulfilment of the promises in deed most difficult and beyond hope, especially if you sanction the agreement by any oaths. We, therefore, despairing in view of your deception, have been compelled to come before you in arms, and as for you, my dear Romans, consider that from now on you will be obliged to do nothing else than make war against the Persians. For here we shall be compelled either to die or grow old until you accord to us justice in deed." Such was the reply which the mirranes wrote back. And again Belisarius and his generals wrote as follows: "O excellent mirranes, it is not fitting in all things to depend upon boasting, nor to lay upon one's neighbours reproaches which are justified on no grounds whatever. For we said with truth that Rufinus had come to act as an envoy and was not far away, and you yourself will know this at no remote time. But since you are eager for deeds of war, we shall array ourselves against you with the help of God, who will, we know, support us in the danger, being moved by the peaceful inclination of the Romans, but rebuking the boastfulness of the Persians and your decision to resist us when we invite you to peace. And we shall array ourselves against you, having prepared for the conflict by fastening the letters written by each of us on the top of our banners." Such was the message of this letter. And the mirranes again answered as follows: "Neither are we entering upon the war without our gods, and with their help we shall come before you, and I expect that on the morrow they will bring the Persians into Daras. But let the bath and lunch be in readiness for me within the fortifications." When Belisarius and his generals read this, they prepared themselves for the conflict.

On the succeeding day the mirranes called together all the Persians at about sunrise and spoke as follows: "I am not ignorant that it is not because of words of their leaders, but because of their individual bravery and their shame before each other that the Persians are accustomed to be courageous in the presence of dangers. But seeing you considering why in the world it is that, although the Romans have not been accustomed heretofore to go into battle without confusion and disorder, they recently awaited the advancing Persians with a kind of order which is by no means characteristic of them, for this reason I have decided to speak some words of exhortation to you, so that it may not come about that you be deceived by reason of holding an opinion which is not true. For I would not have you think that the Romans have suddenly become better warriors, or that they have acquired any more valour or experience, but that they have become more cowardly than they were previously; at any rate they fear the Persians so much that they have not even dared to form their phalanx without a trench. And not even with this did they begin any fighting, but when we did not join battle with them at all, joyfully and considering that matters had gone better for them than they had hoped, they withdrew to the wall. For this reason too it happened that they were not thrown into confusion, for they had not yet come into the dangers of battle. But if the fighting comes to close quarters, fear will seize upon them, and this, together with their inexperience, will throw them, in all probability, into their customary disorder. Such, therefore, is the case with regard to the enemy; but do you, O men of Persia, call to mind the judgment of the King of Kings. For if you do not play the part of brave men in the present engagement, in a manner worthy of the valour of the Persians, an inglorious punishment will fall upon you." With this exhortation the mirranes began to lead his army against the enemy. Likewise Belisarius and Hermogenes gathered all the Romans before the fortifications, and encouraged them with the following words: "You know assuredly that the Persians are not altogether invincible, nor too strong to be killed, having taken their measure in the previous battle; and that, although superior to them in bravery and in strength of body, you were defeated only by reason of being rather heedless of your officers, no one can deny. This thing you now have the opportunity to set right with no trouble. For while the adversities of fortune are by no means such as to be set right by an effort, reason may easily become for a man a physician for the ills caused by himself. If therefore you are willing to give heed to the orders given, you will straightway win for yourselves the superiority in battle. For the Persians come against us basing their confidence on nothing else than our disorder. But this time also they will be disappointed in this hope, and will depart just as in the previous encounter. And as for the great numbers of the enemy, by which more than anything else they inspire fear, it is right for you to despise them. For their whole infantry is nothing more than a crowd of pitiable peasants who come into battle for no other purpose than to dig through walls and to despoil the slain and in general to serve the soldiers. For this reason they have no weapons at all with which they might trouble their opponents, and they only hold before themselves those enormous shields in order that they may not possibly be hit by the enemy. Therefore if you shew yourselves brave men in this struggle, you will not only conquer the Persians for the present, but you will also punish them for their folly, so that they will never again make an expedition into the Roman territory."

When Belisarius and Hermogenes had finished this exhortation, since they saw the Persians advancing against them, they hastily drew up the soldiers in the same manner as before. And the barbarians, coming up before them, took their stand facing the Romans. But the mirranes did not array all the Persians against the enemy, but only one half of them, while he allowed the others to remain behind. These were to take the places of the men who were fighting and to fall upon their opponents with their vigour intact, so that all might fight in constant rotation. But the detachment of the so-called Immortals alone he ordered to remain at rest until he himself should give the signal. And he took his own station at the middle of the front, putting Pityaxes in command on the right wing, and Baresmanas on the left. In this manner, then, both armies were drawn up. Then Pharas came before Belisarius and Hermogenes, and said: "It does not seem to me that I shall do the enemy any great harm if I remain here with the Eruli; but if we conceal ourselves on this slope, and then, when the Persians have begun the fight, if we climb up by this hill and suddenly come upon their rear, shooting from behind them, we shall in all probability do them the greatest harm." Thus he spoke, and, since it pleased Belisarius and his staff, he carried out this plan.

But up to midday neither side began battle. As soon, however, as the noon hour was passed, the barbarians began the fight, having postponed the engagement to this time of the day for the reason that they are accustomed to partake of food only towards late afternoon, while the Romans have their meal before noon; and for this reason they thought that the Romans would never hold out so well, if they assailed them while hungry. At first, then, both sides discharged arrows against each other, and the missiles by their great number made, as it were, a vast cloud; and many men were falling on both sides, but the missiles of the barbarians flew much more thickly. For fresh men were always fighting in turn, affording to their enemy not the slightest opportunity to observe what was being done; but even so the Romans did not have the worst of it. For a steady wind blew from their side against the barbarians, and checked to a considerable degree the force of their arrows. Then, after both sides had exhausted all their missiles, they began to use their spears against each other, and the battle had come still more to close quarters. On the Roman side the left wing was suffering especially. For the Cadiseni, who with Pityaxes were fighting at this point, rushing up suddenly in great numbers, routed their enemy, and crowding hard upon the fugitives, were killing many of them. When this was observed by the men under Sunicas and Aigan, they charged against them at full speed. But first the three hundred Eruli under Pharas from the high ground got in the rear of the enemy and made a wonderful display of valorous deeds against all of them and especially the Cadiseni. And the Persians, seeing the forces of Sunicas too already coming up against them from the flank, turned to a hasty flight. And the rout became complete, for the Romans here joined forces with each other, and there was a great slaughter of the barbarians. On the Persian right wing not fewer than three thousand perished in this action, while the rest escaped with difficulty to the phalanx and were saved. And the Romans did not continue their pursuit, but both sides took their stand facing each other in line. Such was the course of these events.

But the mirranes stealthily sent to the left a large body of troops and with them all the so-called Immortals. And when these were noticed by Belisarius and Hermogenes, they ordered the six hundred men under Sunicas and Aigan to go to the angle on the right, where the troops of Simmas and Ascan were stationed, and behind them they placed many of Belisarius men. So the Persians who held the left wing under the leadership of Baresmanas, together with the Immortals, charged on the run upon the Romans opposite them, who failed to withstand the attack and beat a hasty retreat. Thereupon the Romans in the angle, and all who were behind them, advanced with great ardour against the pursuers. But inasmuch as they came upon the barbarians from the side, they cut their army into two parts, and the greater portion of them they had on their right, while some also who were left behind were placed on their left. Among these happened to be the standard bearer of Baresmanas, whom Sunicas charged and struck with his spear. And already the Persians who were leading the pursuit perceived in what straits they were, and, wheeling about, they stopped the pursuit and went against their assailants, and thus became exposed to the enemy on both sides. For those in flight before them understood what was happening and turned back again. The Persians, on their part, with the detachment of the Immortals, seeing the standard inclined and lowered to the earth, rushed all together against the Romans at that point with Baresmanas. There the Romans held their ground. And first Sunicas killed Baresmanas and threw him from his horse to the ground. As a result of this the barbarians were seized with great fear and thought no longer of resistance, but fled in utter confusion. And the Romans, having made a circle as it were around them, killed about five thousand. Thus both armies were all set in motion, the Persians in retreat, and the Romans in pursuit. In this part of the conflict all the foot-soldiers who were in the Persian army threw down their shields and were caught and wantonly killed by their enemy. However, the pursuit was not continued by the Romans over a great distance. For Belisarius and Hermogenes refused absolutely to let them go farther, fearing lest the Persians through some necessity should turn about and rout them while pursuing recklessly, and it seemed to them sufficient to preserve the victory unmarred. For on that day the Persians had been defeated in battle by the Romans, a thing which had not happened for a long time. Thus the two armies separated from each other. And the Persians were no longer willing to fight a pitched battle with the Romans. However, some sudden attacks were made on both sides, in which the Romans were not at a disadvantage. Such, then, was the fortune of the armies in Mesopotamia.

XV

And Cabades sent another army into the part of Armenia which is subject to the Romans. This army was composed of Persarmenians and Sunitae, whose land adjoins that of the Alani. There were also Huns with them, of the stock called Sabiri, to the number of three thousand, a most warlike race. And Mermeroes, a Persian, had been made general of the whole force. When this army was three days' march from Theodosiopolis, they established their camp and, remaining in the land of the Persarmenians, made their preparations for the invasion. Now the general of Armenia was, as it happened, Dorotheus, a man of discretion and experienced in many wars. And Sittas held the office of general in Byzantium, and had authority over the whole army in Armenia. These two, then, upon learning that an army was being assembled in Persarmenia, straightway sent two body-guards with instructions to spy out the whole force of the enemy and report to them. And both of these men got into the barbarian camp, and after noting everything accurately, they departed. And they were travelling toward some place in that region, when they happened unexpectedly upon hostile Huns. By them one of the two, Dagaris by name, was made captive and bound, while the other succeeded in escaping and reported everything to the generals. They then armed their whole force and made an unexpected assault upon the camp of their enemy; and the barbarians, panic-stricken by the unexpected attack, never thought of resistance, but fled as best each one could. Thereupon the Romans, after killing a large number and plundering the camp, immediately marched back.

Not long after this Mermeroes, having collected the whole army, invaded the Roman territory, and they came upon their enemy near the city of Satala. There they established themselves in camp and remained at rest in a place called Octava, which is fifty-six stades distant from the city. Sittas therefore led out a thousand men and concealed them behind one of the many hills which surround the plain in which the city of Satala lies. Dorotheus with the rest of the army he ordered to stay inside the fortifications, because they thought that they were by no means able to withstand the enemy on level ground, since their number was not fewer than thirty thousand, while their own forces scarcely amounted to half that number. On the following day the barbarians came up close to the fortifications and busily set about closing in the town. But suddenly, seeing the forces of Sittas who by now were coming down upon them from the high ground, and having no means of estimating their number, since owing to the summer season a great cloud of dust hung over them, they thought they were much more numerous than they were, and, hurriedly abandoning their plan of closing in the town, they hastened to mass their force into a small space. But the Romans anticipated the movement and, separating their own force into two detachments, they set upon them as they were retiring from the fortifications; and when this was seen by the whole Roman army, they took courage, and with a great rush they poured out from the fortifications and advanced against their opponents. They thus put the Persians between their own troops, and turned them to flight. However, since the barbarians were greatly superior to their enemy in numbers, as has been said, they still offered resistance, and the battle had become a fierce fight at close quarters. And both sides kept making advances upon their opponents and retiring quickly, for they were all cavalry. Thereupon Florentius, a Thracian, commanding a detachment of horse, charged into the enemy's centre, and seizing the general's standard, forced it to the ground, and started to ride back. And though he himself was overtaken and fell there, hacked to pieces, he proved to be the chief cause of the victory for the Romans. For when the barbarians no longer saw the standard, they were thrown into great confusion and terror, and retreating, got inside their camp, and remained quiet, having lost many men in the battle; and on the following day they all returned homeward with no one following them up, for it seemed to the Romans a great and very noteworthy thing that such a great multitude of barbarians in their own country had suffered those things which have just been narrated above, and that, after making an invasion into hostile territory, they should retire thus without accomplishing anything and defeated by a smaller force.

At that time the Romans also acquired certain Persian strongholds in Persarmenia, both the fortress of Bolum and the fortress called Pharangium, which is the place where the Persians mine gold, which they take to the king. It happened also that a short time before this they had reduced to subjection the Tzanic nation, who had been settled from of old in Roman territory as an autonomous people; and as to these things, the manner in which they were accomplished will be related here and now.

As one goes from the land of Armenia into Persarmenia the Taurus lies on the right, extending into Iberia and the peoples there, as has been said a little before this[19], while on the left the road which continues to descend for a great distance is overhung by exceedingly precipitous mountains, concealed forever by clouds and snow, from which the Phasis River issues and flows into the land of Colchis. In this place from the beginning lived barbarians, the Tzanic nation, subject to no one, called Sani in early times; they made plundering expeditions among the Romans who lived round about, maintaining a most difficult existence, and always living upon what they stole; for their land produced for them nothing good to eat. Wherefore also the Roman emperor sent them each year a fixed amount of gold, with the condition that they should never plunder the country thereabout. And the barbarians had sworn to observe this agreement with the oaths peculiar to their nation, and then, disregarding what they had sworn, they had been accustomed for a long time to make unexpected attacks and to injure not only the Armenians, but also the Romans who lived next to them as far as the sea; then, after completing their inroad in a short space of time, they would immediately betake themselves again to their homes. And whenever it so happened that they chanced upon a Roman army, they were always defeated in the battle, but they proved to be absolutely beyond capture owing to the strength of their fastnesses. In this way Sittas had defeated them in battle before this war; and then by many manifestations of kindness in word and in deed he had been able to win them over completely. For they changed their manner of life to one of a more civilized sort, and enrolled themselves among the Roman troops, and from that time they have gone forth against the enemy with the rest of the Roman army. They also abandoned their own religion for a more righteous faith, and all of them became Christians. Such then was the history of the Tzani.

Beyond the borders of this people there is a cañon whose walls are both high and exceedingly steep, extending as far as the Caucasus mountains. In it are populous towns, and grapes and other fruits grow plentifully. And this canon for about the space of a three days' journey is tributary to the Romans, but from there begins the territory of Persarmenia; and here is the gold-mine which, with the permission of Cabades, was worked by one of the natives, Symeon by name. When this Symeon saw that both nations were actively engaged in the war, he decided to deprive Cabades of the revenue. Therefore he gave over both himself and Pharangium to the Romans, but refused to deliver over to either one the gold of the mine. And as for the Romans, they did nothing, thinking it sufficient for them that the enemy had lost the income from there, and the Persians were not able against the will of the Romans to force the inhabitants of the place to terms, because they were baffled by the difficult country.

At about the same time Narses and Aratius who at the beginning of this war, as I have stated above,[20] had an encounter with Sittas and Belisarius in the land of the Persarmenians, came together with their mother as deserters to the Romans; and the emperor's steward, Narses, received them (for he too happened to be a Persarmenian by birth), and he presented them with a large sum of money. When this came to the knowledge of Isaac, their youngest brother, he secretly opened negotiations with the Romans, and delivered over to them the fortress of Bolum, which lies very near the limits of Theodosiopolis. For he directed that soldiers should be concealed somewhere in the vicinity, and he received them into the fort by night, opening stealthily one small gate for them. Thus he too came to Byzantium.

XVI

Thus matters stood with the Romans. But the Persians, though defeated by Belisarius in the battle at Daras, refused even so to retire from there, until Rufinus, coming into the presence of Cabades, spoke as follows: "O King, I have been sent by thy brother, who reproaches thee with a just reproach, because the Persians for no righteous cause have come in arms into his land. But it would be more seemly for a king who is not only mighty, but also wise as thou art, to secure a peaceful conclusion of war, rather than, when affairs have been satisfactorily settled, to inflict upon himself and his people unnecessary confusion. Wherefore also I myself have come here with good hopes, in order that from now on both peoples may enjoy the blessings which come from peace." So spoke Rufinus. And Cabades replied as follows: "O son of Silvanus, by no means try to reverse the causes, understanding as you do best of all men that you Romans have been the chief cause of the whole confusion. For we have taken the Caspian Gates to the advantage of both Persians and Romans, after forcing out the barbarians there, since Anastasius, the Emperor of the Romans, as you yourself doubtless know, when the opportunity was offered him to buy them with money, was not willing to do so, in order that he might not be compelled to squander great sums of money in behalf of both nations by keeping an army there perpetually. And since that time we have stationed that great army there, and have supported it up to the present time, thereby giving you the privilege of inhabiting the land unplundered as far as concerns the barbarians on that side, and of holding your own possessions with complete freedom from trouble. But as if this were not sufficient for you, you have also made a great city, Daras, as a stronghold against the Persians, although this was explicitly forbidden in the treaty which Anatolius arranged with the Persians; and as a result of this it is necessary for the Persian state to be afflicted with the difficulties and the expense of two armies, the one in order that the Massagetae may not be able fearlessly to plunder the land of both of us, and the other in order that we may check your inroads. When lately we made a protest regarding these matters and demanded that one of two things should be done by you, either that the army sent to the Caspian Gates should be sent by both of us, or that the city of Daras should be dismantled, you refused to understand what was said, but saw fit to strengthen your plot against the Persians by a greater injury, if we remember correctly the building of the fort in Mindouos[21]. And even now the Romans may choose peace, or they may elect war, by either doing justice to us or going against our rights. For never will the Persians lay down their arms, until the Romans either help them in guarding the gates, as is just and right, or dismantle the city of Daras." With these words Cabades dismissed the ambassador, dropping the hint that he was willing to take money from the Romans and have done with the causes of the war. This was reported to the emperor by Rufinus when he came to Byzantium. [531 A.D.] Hermogenes also came thither not long afterwards, and the winter came to a close; thus ended the fourth year of the reign of the Emperor Justinian.

XVII

At the opening of spring a Persian army under the leadership of Azarethes invaded the Roman territory. They were fifteen thousand strong, all horsemen. With them was Alamoundaras, son of Saccice, with a very large body of Saracens. But this invasion was not made by the Persians in the customary manner; for they did not invade Mesopotamia, as formerly, but the country called Commagene of old, but now Euphratesia, a point from which, as far as we know, the Persians never before conducted a campaign against the Romans. But why the land was called Mesopotamia and why the Persians refrained from making their attack at this point is what I now propose to relate.

There is a mountain in Armenia which is not especially precipitous, two-and-forty stadés removed from Theodosiopolis and lying toward the north from it. From this mountain issue two springs, forming immediately two rivers, the one on the right called the Euphrates, and the other the Tigris. One of these, the Tigris, descends, with no deviations and with no tributaries except small ones emptying into it, straight toward the city of Amida. And continuing into the country which lies to the north of this city it enters the land of Assyria. But the Euphrates at its beginning flows for a short distance, and is then immediately lost to sight as it goes on; it does not, however, become subterranean, but a very strange thing happens. For the water is covered by a bog of great depth, extending about fifty stades in length and twenty in breadth; and reeds grow in this mud in great abundance. But the earth there is of such a hard sort that it seems to those who chance upon it to be nothing else than solid ground, so that both pedestrians and horsemen travel over it without any fear. Nay more, even wagons pass over the place in great numbers every day, but they are wholly insufficient to shake the bog or to find a weak spot in it at any point. The natives burn the reeds every year, to prevent the roads being stopped up by them, and once, when an exceedingly violent wind struck the place, it came about that the fire reached the extremities of the roots, and the water appeared at a small opening; but in a short time the ground closed again, and gave the spot the same appearance which it had had before. From there the river proceeds into the land called Celesene, where was the sanctuary of Artemis among the Taurians, from which they say Iphigenia, daughter of Agamemnon, fled with Orestes and Pylades, bearing the statue of Artemis. For the other temple which has existed even to my day in the city of Comana is not the one "Among the Taurians." But I shall explain how this temple came into being.

When Orestes had departed in haste from the Taurians with his sister, it so happened that he contracted some disease. And when he made inquiry about the disease they say that the oracle responded that his trouble would not abate until he built a temple to Artemis in a spot such as the one among the Taurians, and there cut off his hair and named the city after it. So then Orestes, going about the country there, came to Pontus, and saw a mountain which rose steep and towering, while below along the extremities of the mountain flowed the river Iris. Orestes, therefore, supposing at that time that this was the place indicated to him by the oracle, built there a great city and the temple of Artemis, and, shearing off his hair, named after it the city which even up to the present time has been called Comana. The story goes on that after Orestes had done these things, the disease continued to be as violent as before, if not even more so. Then the man perceived that he was not satisfying the oracle by doing these things, and he again went about looking everywhere and found a certain spot in Cappadocia very closely resembling the one among the Taurians. I myself have often seen this place and admired it exceedingly, and have imagined that I was in the land of the Taurians. For this mountain resembles the other remarkably, since the Taurus is here also and the river Sarus is similar to the Euphrates there. So Orestes built in that place an imposing city and two temples, the one to Artemis and the other to his sister Iphigenia, which the Christians have made sanctuaries for themselves, without changing their structure at all. This is called even now Golden Comana, being named from the hair of Orestes, which they say he cut off there and thus escaped from his affliction. But some say that this disease from which he escaped was nothing else than that of madness which seized him after he had killed his own mother. But I shall return to the previous narrative.

From Tauric Armenia and the land of Celesene the River Euphrates, flowing to the right of the Tigris, flows around an extensive territory, and since many rivers join it and among them the Arsinus, whose copious stream flows down from the land of the so-called Persarmenians, it becomes naturally a great river, and flows into the land of the people anciently called White Syrians but now known as the Lesser Armenians, whose first city, Melitene, is one of great importance. From there it flows past Samosata and Hierapolis and all the towns in that region as far as the land of Assyria, where the two rivers unite with each other into one stream which bears the name of the Tigris. The land which lies outside the River Euphrates, beginning with Samosata, was called in ancient times Commagene, but now it is named after the river[22]. But the land inside the river, that namely which is between it and the Tigris, is appropriately named Mesopotamia; however, a portion of it is called not only by this name, but also by certain others. For the land as far as the city of Amida has come to be called Armenia by some, while Edessa together with the country around it is called Osroene, after Osroes, a man who was king in that place in former times, when the men of this country were in alliance with the Persians. After the time, therefore, when the Persians had taken from the Romans the city of Nisibis and certain other places in Mesopotamia, whenever they were about to make an expedition against the Romans, they disregarded the land outside the River Euphrates, which was for the most part unwatered and deserted by men, and gathered themselves here with no trouble, since they were in a land which was their own and which lay very close to the inhabited land of their enemy, and from here they always made their invasions.

When the mirranes[23], defeated in battle[24] and with the greater part of his men lost, came back to the Persian land with the remainder of his army, he received bitter punishment at the hands of King Cabades. For he took away from him a decoration which he was accustomed to bind upon the hair of his head, an ornament wrought of gold and pearls. Now this is a great dignity among the Persians, second only to the kingly honour. For there it is unlawful to wear a gold ring or girdle or brooch or anything else whatsoever, except a man be counted worthy to do so by the king.

Thereafter Cabades began to consider in what manner he himself should make an expedition against the Romans. For after the mirranes had failed in the manner I have told, he felt confidence in no one else. While he was completely at a loss as to what he should do, Alamoundaras, the king of the Saracens, came before him and said: "Not everything, O Master, should be entrusted to fortune, nor should one believe that all wars ought to be successful. For this is not likely and besides it is not in keeping with the course of human events, but this idea is most unfortunate for those who are possessed by it. For when men who expect that all the good things will come to them fail at any time, if it so happen, they are distressed more than is seemly by the very hope which wrongly led them on. Therefore, since men have not always confidence in fortune, they do not enter into the danger of war in a straightforward way, even if they boast that they surpass the enemy in every respect, but by deception and divers devices they exert themselves to circumvent their opponents. For those who assume the risk of an even struggle have no assurance of victory. Now, therefore, O King of Kings, neither be thus distressed by the misfortune which has befallen Mirranes, nor desire again to make trial of fortune. For in Mesopotamia and the land of Osroene, as it is called, since it is very close to thy boundaries, the cities are very strong above all others, and now they contain a multitude of soldiers such as never before, so that if we go there the contest will not prove a safe one; but in the land which lies outside the River Euphrates, and in Syria which adjoins it, there is neither a fortified city nor an army of any importance. For this I have often heard from the Saracens sent as spies to these parts. There too, they say, is the city of Antioch, in wealth and size and population the first of all the cities of the Eastern Roman Empire; and this city is unguarded and destitute of soldiers. For the people of this city care for nothing else than fêtes and luxurious living, and their constant rivalries with each other in the theatres. Accordingly, if we go against them unexpectedly, it is not at all unlikely that we shall capture the city by a sudden attack, and that we shall return to the land of the Persians without having met any hostile army, and before the troops in Mesopotamia have learned what has happened. As for lack of water or of any kind of provisions, let no such thought occur to thee; for I myself shall lead the army wherever it shall seem best."

When Cabades heard this he could neither oppose nor distrust the plan. For Alamoundaras was most discreet and well experienced in matters of warfare, thoroughly faithful to the Persians, and unusually energetic, a man who for a space of fifty years forced the Roman state to bend the knee. For beginning from the boundaries of Aegypt and as far as Mesopotamia he plundered the whole country, pillaging one place after another, burning the buildings in his track and making captives of the population by the tens of thousands on each raid, most of whom he killed without consideration, while he gave up the others for great sums of money. And he was confronted by no one at all. For he never made his inroad without looking about, but so suddenly did he move and so very opportunely for himself, that, as a rule, he was already off with all the plunder when the generals and the soldiers were beginning to learn what had happened and to gather themselves against him. If, indeed, by any chance, they were able to catch him, this barbarian would fall upon his pursuers while still unprepared and not in battle array, and would rout and destroy them with no trouble; and on one occasion he made prisoners of all the soldiers who were pursuing him together with their officers. These officers were Timostratus, the brother of Rufinus, and John, the son of Lucas, whom he gave up indeed later, thereby gaining for himself no mean or trivial wealth. And, in a word, this man proved himself the most difficult and dangerous enemy of all to the Romans. The reason was this, that Alamoundaras, holding the position of king, ruled alone over all the Saracens in Persia, and he was always able to make his inroad with the whole army wherever he wished in the Roman domain; and neither any commander of Roman troops, whom they call "duces," nor any leader of the Saracens allied with the Romans, who are called "phylarchs," was strong enough with his men to array himself against Alamoundaras; for the troops stationed in the different districts were not a match in battle for the enemy. [531 A.D.] For this reason the Emperor Justinian put in command of as many clans as possible Arethas, the son of Gabalas, who ruled over the Saracens of Arabia, and bestowed upon him the dignity of king, a thing which among the Romans had never before been done. However Alamoundaras continued to injure the Romans just as much as before, if not more, since Arethas was either extremely unfortunate in every inroad and every conflict, or else he turned traitor as quickly as he could. For as yet we know nothing certain about him. In this way it came about that Alamoundaras, with no one to stand against him, plundered the whole East for an exceedingly long time, for he lived to a very advanced age.

XVIII

This man's suggestion at that time therefore pleased Cabades, and he chose out fifteen thousand men, putting in command of them Azarethes, a Persian, who was an exceptionally able warrior, and he bade Alamoundaras lead the expedition. So they crossed the River Euphrates in Assyria, and, after passing over some uninhabited country, they suddenly and unexpectedly threw their forces into the land of the so-called Commagenae. This was the first invasion made by the Persians from this point into Roman soil, as far as we know from tradition or by any other means, and it paralyzed all the Romans with fear by its unexpectedness. And when this news came to the knowledge of Belisarius, at first he was at a loss, but afterwards he decided to go to the rescue with all speed. So he established a sufficient garrison in each city in order that Cabades with another hostile army might not come there and find the towns of Mesopotamia utterly unguarded, and himself with the rest of the army went to meet the invasion; and crossing the River Euphrates they moved forward in great haste. Now the Roman army amounted to about twenty thousand foot and horse, and among them not less than two thousand were Isaurians. The commanders of cavalry were all the same ones who had previously fought the battle at Daras with Mirranes and the Persians, while the infantry were commanded by one of the body-guards of the Emperor Justinian, Peter by name. The Isaurians, however, were under the command of Longinus and Stephanacius. Arethas also came there to join them with the Saracen army. When they reached the city of Chalcis, they encamped and remained there, since they learned that the enemy were in a place called Gabboulon, one hundred and ten stades away from Chalcis. When this became known to Alamoundaras and Azarethes, they were terrified at the danger, and no longer continued their advance, but decided to retire homeward instantly. Accordingly they began to march back, with the River Euphrates on the left, while the Roman army was following in the rear. And in the spot where the Persians bivouacked each night the Romans always tarried on the following night. For Belisarius purposely refused to allow the army to make any longer march because he did not wish to come to an engagement with the enemy, but he considered that it was sufficient for them that the Persians and Alamoundaras, after invading the land of the Romans, should retire from it in such a fashion, betaking themselves to their own land without accomplishing anything. And because of this all secretly mocked him, both officers and soldiers, but not a man reproached him to his face.

Finally the Persians made their bivouac on the bank of the Euphrates just opposite the city of Callinicus. From there they were about to march through a country absolutely uninhabited by man, and thus to quit the land of the Romans; for they purposed no longer to proceed as before, keeping to the bank of the river. The Romans had passed the night in the city of Sura, and, removing from there, they came upon the enemy just in the act of preparing for the departure. [Ap. 19, 531] Now the feast of Easter was near and would take place on the following day; this feast is reverenced by the Christians above all others, and on the day before it they are accustomed to refrain from food and drink not only throughout the day, but for a large part of the night also they continue the fast. Then, therefore, Belisarius, seeing that all his men were passionately eager to go against the enemy, wished to persuade them to give up this idea (for this course had been counselled by Hermogenes also, who had come recently on an embassy from the emperor); he accordingly called together all who were present and spoke as follows: "O Romans, whither are you rushing? and what has happened to you that you are purposing to choose for yourselves a danger which is not necessary? Men believe that there is only one victory which is unalloyed, namely to suffer no harm at the hands of the enemy, and this very thing has been given us in the present instance by fortune and by the fear of us that overpowers our foes. Therefore it is better to enjoy the benefit of our present blessings than to seek them when they have passed. For the Persians, led on by many hopes, undertook an expedition against the Romans, and now, with everything lost, they have beaten a hasty retreat. So that if we compel them against their will to abandon their purpose of withdrawing and to come to battle with us, we shall win no advantage whatsoever if we are victorious, for why should one rout a fugitive? while if we are unfortunate, as may happen, we shall both be deprived of the victory which we now have, not robbed of it by the enemy, but flinging it away ourselves, and also we shall abandon the land of the emperor to lie open hereafter to the attacks of the enemy without defenders. Moreover this also is worth your consideration, that God is always accustomed to succour men in dangers which are necessary, not in those which they choose for themselves. And apart from this it will come about that those who have nowhere to turn will play the part of brave men even against their will, while the obstacles which are to be met by us in entering the engagement are many; for a large number of you have come on foot and all of us are fasting. I refrain from mentioning that some even now have not arrived." So spoke Belisarius.

But the army began to insult him, not in silence nor with any concealment, but they came shouting into his presence, and called him weak and a destroyer of their zeal; and even some of the officers joined with the soldiers in this offence, thus displaying the extent of their daring. And Belisarius, in astonishment at their shamelessness, changed his exhortation and now seemed to be urging them on against the enemy and drawing them up for battle, saying that he had not known before their eagerness to fight, but that now he was of good courage and would go against the enemy with a better hope. He then formed the phalanx with a single front, disposing his men as follows: on the left wing by the river he stationed all the infantry, while on the right where the ground rose sharply he placed Arethas and all his Saracens; he himself with the cavalry took his position in the centre. Thus the Romans arrayed themselves. And when Azarethes saw the enemy gathering in battle line, he exhorted his men with the following words: "Persians as you are, no one would deny that you would not give up your valour in exchange for life, if a choice of the two should be offered. But I say that not even if you should wish, is it within your power to make the choice between the two. For as for men who have the opportunity to escape from danger and live in dishonour it is not at all unnatural that they should, if they wish, choose what is most pleasant instead of what is best; but for men who are bound to die, either gloriously at the hands of the enemy or shamefully led to punishment by your Master, it is extreme folly not to choose what is better instead of what is most shameful. Now, therefore, when things stand thus, I consider that it befits you all to bear in mind not only the enemy but also your own Lord and so enter this battle."

After Azarethes also had uttered these words of exhortation, he stationed the phalanx opposite his opponents, assigning the Persians the right wing and the Saracens the left. Straightway both sides began the fight, and the battle was exceedingly fierce. For the arrows, shot from either side in very great numbers, caused great loss of life in both armies, while some placed themselves in the interval between the armies and made a display of valorous deeds against each other, and especially among the Persians they were falling by the arrows in great numbers. For while their missiles were incomparably more frequent, since the Persians are almost all bowmen and they learn to make their shots much more rapidly than any other men, still the bows which sent the arrows were weak and not very tightly strung, so that their missiles, hitting a corselet, perhaps, or helmet or shield of a Roman warrior, were broken off and had no power to hurt the man who was hit. The Roman bowmen are always slower indeed, but inasmuch as their bows are extremely stiff and very tightly strung, and one might add that they are handled by stronger men, they easily slay much greater numbers of those they hit than do the Persians, for no armour proves an obstacle to the force of their arrows. Now already two-thirds of the day had passed, and the battle was still even. Then by mutual agreement all the best of the Persian army advanced to attack the Roman right wing, where Arethas and the Saracens had been stationed. But they broke their formation and moved apart, so that they got the reputation of having betrayed the Romans to the Persians. For without awaiting the oncoming enemy they all straightway beat a hasty retreat. So the Persians in this way broke through the enemy's line and immediately got in the rear of the Roman cavalry. Thus the Romans, who were already exhausted both by the march and the labour of the battle, and besides this they were all fasting so far on in the day, now that they were assailed by the enemy on both sides, held out no longer, but the most of them in full flight made their way to the islands in the river which were close by, while some also remained there and performed deeds both amazing and remarkable against the enemy. Among these was Ascan who, after killing many of the notables among the Persians, was gradually hacked to pieces and finally fell, leaving to the enemy abundant reason to remember him. And with him eight hundred others perished after shewing themselves brave men in this struggle, and almost all the Isaurians fell with their leaders, without even daring to lift their weapons against the enemy. For they were thoroughly inexperienced in this business, since they had recently left off farming and entered into the perils of warfare, which before that time were unknown to them. And yet just before these very men had been most furious of all for battle because of their ignorance of warfare, and were then reproaching Belisarius with cowardice. They were not in fact all Isaurians but the majority of them were Lycaones.

Belisarius with some few men remained there, and as long as he saw Ascan and his men holding out, he also in company with those who were with him held back the enemy; but when some of Ascan's troops had fallen, and the others had turned to flee wherever they could, then at length he too fled with his men and came to the phalanx of infantry, who with Peter were still fighting, although not many in number now, since the most of them too had fled. There he himself gave up his horse and commanded all his men to do the same thing and on foot with the others to fight off the oncoming enemy. And those of the Persians who were following the fugitives, after pursuing for only a short distance, straightway returned and rushed upon the infantry and Belisarius with all the others. Then the Romans turned their backs to the river so that no movement to surround them might be executed by the enemy, and as best they could under the circumstances were defending themselves against their assailants. And again the battle became fierce, although the two sides were not evenly matched in strength; for foot-soldiers, and a very few of them, were fighting against the whole Persian cavalry. Nevertheless the enemy were not able either to rout them or in any other way to overpower them. For standing shoulder to shoulder they kept themselves constantly massed in a small space, and they formed with their shields a rigid, unyielding barricade, so that they shot at the Persians more conveniently than they were shot at by them. Many a time after giving up, the Persians would advance against them determined to break up and destroy their line, but they always retired again from the assault unsuccessful. For their horses, annoyed by the clashing of the shields, reared up and made confusion for themselves and their riders. Thus both sides continued the struggle until it had become late in the day. And when night had already come on, the Persians withdrew to their camp, and Belisarius accompanied by some few men found a freight-boat and crossed over to the island in the river, while the other Romans reached the same place by swimming. On the following day many freight-boats were brought to the Romans from the city of Callinicus and they were conveyed thither in them, and the Persians, after despoiling the dead, all departed homeward. However they did not find their own dead less numerous than the enemy's.

When Azarethes reached Persia with his army, although he had prospered in the battle, he found Cabades exceedingly ungrateful, for the following reason. It is a custom among the Persians that, when they are about to march against any of their foes, the king sits on the royal throne, and many baskets are set there before him; and the general also is present who is expected to lead the army against the enemy; then the army passes along before the king, one man at a time, and each of them throws one weapon into the baskets; after this they are sealed with the king's seal and preserved; and when this army returns to Persia, each one of the soldiers takes one weapon out of the baskets. A count is then made by those whose office it is to do so of all the weapons which have not been taken by the men, and they report to the king the number of the soldiers who have not returned, and in this way it becomes evident how many have perished in the war. Thus the law has stood from of old among the Persians. Now when Azarethes came into the presence of the king, Cabades enquired of him whether he came back with any Roman fortress won over to their side, for he had marched forth with Alamoundaras against the Romans, with the purpose of subduing Antioch. And Azarethes said that he had captured no fortress, but that he had conquered the Romans and Belisarius in battle. So Cabades bade the army of Azarethes pass by, and from the baskets each man took out a weapon just as was customary. But since many weapons were left, Cabades rebuked Azarethes for the victory and thereafter ranked him among the most unworthy. So the victory had this conclusion for Azarethes.

XIX

At that time the idea occurred to the Emperor Justinian to ally with himself the Aethiopians and the Homeritae, in order to injure the Persians. I shall now first explain what part of the earth these nations occupy, and then I shall point out in what manner the emperor hoped that they would be of help to the Romans. The boundaries of Palestine extend toward the east to the sea which is called the Red Sea. Now this sea, beginning at India, comes to an end at this point in the Roman domain. And there is a city called Aelas on its shore, where the sea comes to an end, as I have said, and becomes a very narrow gulf. And as one sails into the sea from there, the Egyptian mountains lie on the right, extending toward the south; on the other side a country deserted by men extends northward to an indefinite distance; and the land on both sides is visible as one sails in as far as the island called Iotabe, not less than one thousand stades distant from the city of Aelas. On this island Hebrews had lived from of old in autonomy, but in the reign of this Justinian they have become subject to the Romans. From there on there comes a great open sea. And those who sail into this part of it no longer see the land on the right, but they always anchor along the left coast when night comes on. For it is impossible to navigate in the darkness on this sea, since it is everywhere full of shoals. But there are harbours there and great numbers of them, not made by the hand of man, but by the natural contour of the land, and for this reason it is not difficult for mariners to find anchorage wherever they happen to be.

This coast[25] immediately beyond the boundaries of Palestine is held by Saracens, who have been settled from of old in the Palm Groves. These groves are in the interior, extending over a great tract of land, and there absolutely nothing else grows except palm trees. The Emperor Justinian had received these palm groves as a present from Abochorabus, the ruler of the Saracens there, and he was appointed by the emperor captain over the Saracens in Palestine. And he guarded the land from plunder constantly, for both to the barbarians over whom he ruled and no less to the enemy, Abochorabus always seemed a man to be feared and an exceptionally energetic fellow. Formally, therefore, the emperor holds the Palm Groves, but for him really to possess himself of any of the country there is utterly impossible. For a land completely destitute of human habitation and extremely dry lies between, extending to the distance of a ten days' journey; moreover the Palm Groves themselves are by no means worth anything, and Abochorabus only gave the form of a gift, and the emperor accepted it with full knowledge of the fact. So much then for the Palm Groves. Adjoining this people there are other Saracens in possession of the coast, who are called Maddeni and who are subjects of the Homeritae. These Homeritae dwell in the land on the farther side of them on the shore of the sea. And beyond them many other nations are said to be settled as far as the man-eating Saracens. Beyond these are the nations of India. But regarding these matters let each one speak as he may wish.

About opposite the Homeritae on the opposite mainland dwell the Aethiopians who are called Auxomitae, because their king resides in the city of Auxomis. And the expanse of sea which lies between is crossed in a voyage of five days and nights, when a moderately favouring wind blows. For here they are accustomed to navigate by night also, since there are no shoals at all in these parts; this portion of the sea has been called the Red Sea by some. For the sea which one traverses beyond this point as far as the shore and the city of Aelas has received the name of the Arabian Gulf, inasmuch as the country which extends from here to the limits of the city of Gaza used to be called in olden times Arabia, since the king of the Arabs had his palace in early times in the city of Petrae. Now the harbour of the Homeritae from which they are accustomed to put to sea for the voyage to Aethiopia is called Bulicas; and at the end of the sail across the sea they always put in at the harbour of the Adulitae. But the city of Adulis is removed from the harbour a distance of twenty stades (for it lacks only so much of being on the sea), while from the city of Auxomis it is a journey of twelve days.

All the boats which are found in India and on this sea are not made in the same manner as are other ships. For neither are they smeared with pitch, nor with any other substance, nor indeed are the planks fastened together by iron nails going through and through, but they are bound together with a kind of cording. The reason is not as most persons suppose, that there are certain rocks there which draw the iron to themselves (for witness the fact that when the Roman vessels sail from Aelas into this sea, although they are fitted with much iron, no such thing has ever happened to them), but rather because the Indians and the Aethiopians possess neither iron nor any other thing suitable for such purposes. Furthermore, they are not even able to buy any of these things from the Romans since this is explicitly forbidden to all by law; for death is the punishment for one who is caught. Such then is the description of the so-called Red Sea[26] and of the land which lies on either side of it.

From the city of Auxomis to the Aegyptian boundaries of the Roman domain, where the city called Elephantine is situated, is a journey of thirty days for an unencumbered traveller. Within that space many nations are settled, and among them the Blemyes and the Nobatae, who are very large nations. But the Blemyes dwell in the central portion of the country, while the Nobatae possess the territory about the River Nile. Formerly this was not the limit of the Roman empire, but it lay beyond there as far as one would advance in a seven days' journey; but the Roman Emperor Diocletian came there, and observed that the tribute from these places was of the smallest possible account, since the land is at that point extremely narrow (for rocks rise to an exceedingly great height at no great distance from the Nile and spread over the rest of the country), while a very large body of soldiers had been stationed there from of old, the maintenance of which was an excessive burden upon the public; and at the same time the Nobatae who formerly dwelt about the city of Oasis used to plunder the whole region; so he persuaded these barbarians to move from their own habitations, and to settle along the River Nile, promising to bestow upon them great cities and land both extensive and incomparably better than that which they had previously occupied. For in this way he thought that they would no longer harass the country about Oasis at least, and that they would possess themselves of the land given them, as being their own, and would probably beat off the Blemyes and the other barbarians. And since this pleased the Nobatae, they made the migration immediately, just as Diocletian directed them, and took possession of all the Roman cities and the land on both sides of the river beyond the city of Elephantine. Then it was that this emperor decreed that to them and to the Blemyes a fixed sum of gold should be given every year with the stipulation that they should no longer plunder the land of the Romans. And they receive this gold even up to my time, but none the less they overrun the country there. Thus it seems that with all barbarians there is no means of compelling them to keep faith with the Romans except through the fear of soldiers to hold them in check. And yet this emperor went so far as to select a certain island in the River Nile close to the city of Elephantine and there construct a very strong fortress in which he established certain temples and altars for the Romans and these barbarians in common, and he settled priests of both nations in this fortress, thinking that the friendship between them would be secure by reason of their sharing the things sacred to them. And for this reason he named the place Philae. Now both these nations, the Blemyes and the Nobatae, believe in all the gods in which the Greeks believe, and they also reverence Isis and Osiris, and not least of all Priapus. But the Blemyes are accustomed also to sacrifice human beings to the sun. These sanctuaries in Philae were kept by these barbarians even up to my time, but the Emperor Justinian decided to tear them down. Accordingly Narses, a Persarmenian by birth, whom I have mentioned before as having deserted to the Romans[27], being commander of the troops there, tore down the sanctuaries at the emperor's order, and put the priests under guard and sent the statues to Byzantium. But I shall return to the previous narrative.

XX

At about the time of this war Hellestheaeus, the king of the Aethiopians, who was a Christian and a most devoted adherent of this faith, discovered that a number of the Homeritae on the opposite mainland were oppressing the Christians there outrageously; many of these rascals were Jews, and many of them held in reverence the old faith which men of the present day call Hellenic. He therefore collected a fleet of ships and an army and came against them, and he conquered them in battle and slew both the king and many of the Homeritae. He then set up in his stead a Christian king, a Homerite by birth, by name Esimiphaeus, and, after ordaining that he should pay a tribute to the Aethiopians every year, he returned to his home. In this Aethiopian army many slaves and all who were readily disposed to crime were quite unwilling to follow the king back, but were left behind and remained there because of their desire for the land of the Homeritae; for it is an extremely goodly land.

These fellows at a time not long after this, in company with certain others, rose against the king Esimiphaeus and put him in confinement in one of the fortresses there, and established another king over the Homeritae, Abramus by name. Now this Abramus was a Christian, but a slave of a Roman citizen who was engaged in the business of shipping in the city of Adulis in Aethiopia. When Hellestheaeus learned this, he was eager to punish Abramus together with those who had revolted with him for their injustice to Esimiphaeus, and he sent against them an army of three thousand men with one of his relatives as commander. This army, once there, was no longer willing to return home, but they wished to remain where they were in a goodly land, and so without the knowledge of their commander they opened negotiations with Abramus; then when they came to an engagement with their opponents, just as the fighting began, they killed their commander and joined the ranks of the enemy, and so remained there. But Hellestheaeus was greatly moved with anger and sent still another army against them; this force engaged with Abramus and his men, and, after suffering a severe defeat in the battle, straightway returned home. Thereafter the king of the Aethiopians became afraid, and sent no further expeditions against Abramus. After the death of Hellestheaeus, Abramus agreed to pay tribute to the king of the Aethiopians who succeeded him, and in this way he strengthened his rule. But this happened at a later time.

At that time, when Hellestheaeus was reigning over the Aethiopians, and Esimiphaeus over the Homeritae, the Emperor Justinian sent an ambassador, Julianus, demanding that both nations on account of their community of religion should make common cause with the Romans in the war against the Persians; for he purposed that the Aethiopians, by purchasing silk from India and selling it among the Romans, might themselves gain much money, while causing the Romans to profit in only one way, namely, that they be no longer compelled to pay over their money to their enemy. (This is the silk of which they are accustomed to make the garments which of old the Greeks called

Medic, but which at the present time they name "seric"[28]). As for the Homeritae, it was desired that they should establish Caïsus, the fugitive, as captain over the Maddeni, and with a great army of their own people and of the Maddene Saracens make an invasion into the land of the Persians. This Caïsus was by birth of the captain's rank and an exceptionally able warrior, but he had killed one of the relatives of Esimiphaeus and was a fugitive in a land which is utterly destitute of human habitation. So each king, promising to put this demand into effect, dismissed the ambassador, but neither one of them did the things agreed upon by them. For it was impossible for the Aethiopians to buy silk from the Indians, for the Persian merchants always locate themselves at the very harbours where the Indian ships first put in, (since they inhabit the adjoining country), and are accustomed to buy the whole cargoes; and it seemed to the Homeritae a difficult thing to cross a country which was a desert and which extended so far that a long time was required for the journey across it, and then to go against a people much more warlike than themselves. Later on Abramus too, when at length he had established his power most securely, promised the Emperor Justinian many times to invade the land of Persia, but only once began the journey and then straightway turned back. Such then were the relations which the Romans had with the Aethiopians and the Homeritae.

XXI

Hermogenes, as soon as the battle on the Euphrates had taken place, came before Cabades to negotiate with him, but he accomplished nothing regarding the peace on account of which he had come, since he found him still swelling with rage against the Romans; for this reason he returned unsuccessful. And Belisarius came to Byzantium at the summons of the emperor, having been removed from the office which he held, in order that he might march against the Vandals; but Sittas, as had been decreed by the Emperor Justinian, went to the East in order to guard that portion of the empire. And the Persians once more invaded Mesopotamia with a great army under command of Chanaranges and Aspebedes and Mermeroes. Since no one dared to engage with them, they made camp and began the siege of Martyropolis, where Bouzes and Bessas had been stationed in command of the garrison. This city lies in the land called Sophanene, two hundred and forty stades distant from the city of Amida toward the north; it is just on the River Nymphius which divides the land of the Romans and the Persians. So the Persians began to assail the fortifications, and, while the besieged at first withstood them manfully, it did not seem likely that they would hold out long. For the circuit-wall was quite easily assailable in most parts, and could be captured very easily by a Persian siege, and besides they did not have a sufficient supply of provisions, nor indeed had they engines of war nor anything else that was of any value for defending themselves. Meanwhile Sittas and the Roman army came to a place called Attachas, one hundred stades distant from Martyropolis, but they did not dare to advance further, but established their camp and remained there. Hermogenes also was with them, coming again as ambassador from Byzantium. At this point the following event took place.

It has been customary from ancient times both among the Romans and the Persians to maintain spies at public expense; these men are accustomed to go secretly among the enemy, in order that they may investigate accurately what is going on, and may then return and report to the rulers. Many of these men, as is natural, exert themselves to act in a spirit of loyalty to their nation, while some also betray their secrets to the enemy. At that time a certain spy who had been sent from the Persians to the Romans came into the presence of the Emperor Justinian and revealed many things which were taking place among the barbarians, and, in particular, that the nation of the Massagetae, in order to injure the Romans, were on the very point of going out into the land of Persia, and that from there they were prepared to march into the territory of the Romans, and unite with the Persian army. When the emperor heard this, having already a proof of the man's truthfulness to him, he presented him with a handsome sum of money and persuaded him to go to the Persian army which was besieging the Martyropolitans, and announce to the barbarians there that these Massagetae had been won over with money by the Roman emperor, and were about to come against them that very moment. The spy carried out these instructions, and coming to the army of the barbarians he announced to Chanaranges and the others that an army of Huns hostile to them would at no distant time come to the Romans. And when they heard this, they were seized with terror, and were at a loss how to deal with the situation.

At this juncture it came about that Cabades became seriously ill, and he called to him one of the Persians who were in closest intimacy with him, Mebodes by name, and conversed with him concerning Chosroes and the kingdom, and said he feared the Persians would make a serious attempt to disregard some of the things which had been decided upon by him. But Mebodes asked him to leave the declaration of his purpose in writing, and bade him be confident that the Persians would never dare to disregard it. So Cabades set it down plainly that Chosroes should become king over the Persians. The document was written by Mebodes himself, and Cabades immediately passed from among men. [Sept. 13, 531] And when everything had been performed as prescribed by law in the burial of the king, then Caoses, confident by reason of the law, tried to lay claim to the office, but Mebodes stood in his way, asserting that no one ought to assume the royal power by his own initiative but by vote of the Persian notables. So Caoses committed the decision in the matter to the magistrates, supposing that there would be no opposition to him from there. But when all the Persian notables had been gathered together for this purpose and were in session, Mebodes read the document and stated the purpose of Cabades regarding Chosroes, and all, calling to mind the virtue of Cabades, straightway declared Chosroes King of the Persians.

Thus then Chosroes secured the power. But at Martyropolis, Sittas and Hermogenes were in fear concerning the city, since they were utterly unable to defend it in its peril, and they sent certain men to the enemy, who came before the generals and spoke as follows: "It has escaped your own notice that you are becoming wrongfully an obstacle to the king of the Persians and to the blessings of peace and to each state. For ambassadors sent from the emperor are even now present in order that they may go to the king of the Persians and there settle the differences and establish a treaty with him; but do you as quickly as possible remove from the land of the Romans and permit the ambassadors to act in the manner which will be of advantage to both peoples. For we are ready also to give as hostages men of repute concerning these very things, to prove that they will be actually accomplished at no distant date." Such were the words of the ambassadors of the Romans. It happened also that a messenger came to them from the palace, who brought them word that Cabades had died and that Chosroes, son of Cabades, had become king over the Persians, and that in this way the situation had become unsettled. And as a result of this the generals heard the words of the Romans gladly, since they feared also the attack of the Huns. The Romans therefore straightway gave as hostages Martinus and one of the body-guards of Sittas, Senecius by name; so the Persians broke up the siege and made their departure promptly. And the Huns not long afterward invaded the land of the Romans, but since they did not find the Persian army there, they made their raid a short one, and then all departed homeward.

XXII

Straightway Rufinus and Alexander and Thomas came to act as ambassadors with Hermogenes, and they all came before the Persian king at the River Tigris. And when Chosroes saw them, he released the hostages. Then the ambassadors coaxed Chosroes, and spoke many beguiling words most unbecoming to Roman ambassadors. By this treatment Chosroes became tractable, and agreed to establish a peace with them that should be without end for the price of one hundred and ten "centenaria," on condition that the commander of troops in Mesopotamia should be no longer at Daras, but should spend all his time in Constantina, as was customary in former times; but the fortresses in Lazica he refused to give back, although he himself demanded that he should receive back from the Romans both Pharangium and the fortress of Bolum. (Now the "centenarium" weighs one hundred pounds, for which reason it is so called; for the Romans call one hundred "centum"). He demanded that this gold be given him, in order that the Romans might not be compelled either to tear down the city of Daras or to share the garrison at the Caspian Gates with the Persians[29]. However the ambassadors, while approving the rest, said that they were not able to concede the fortresses, unless they should first make enquiry of the emperor concerning them. It was decided, accordingly, that Rufinus should be sent concerning them to Byzantium, and that the others should wait until he should return. And it was arranged with Rufinus that seventy days' time be allowed until he should arrive. When Rufinus reached Byzantium and reported to the emperor what Chosroes' decision was concerning the peace, the emperor commanded that the peace be concluded by them on these terms.

In the meantime, however, a report which was not true reached Persia saying that the Emperor Justinian had become enraged and put Rufinus to death. Chosroes indeed was much perturbed by this, and, already filled with anger, he advanced against the Romans with his whole army. But Rufinus met him on the way as he was returning not far from the city of Nisibis. Therefore they proceeded to this city themselves, and, since they were about to establish the peace, the ambassadors began to convey the money thither. But the Emperor Justinian was already repenting that he had given up the strong holds of Lazica, and he wrote a letter to the ambassadors expressly commanding them by no means to hand them over to the Persians. For this reason Chosroes no longer saw fit to make the treaty; and then it came to the mind of Rufinus that he had counselled more speedily than safely in bringing the money into the land of Persia. Straightway, therefore, he threw himself on the earth, and lying prone he entreated Chosroes to send the money back with them and not march immediately against the Romans, but to put off the war to some other time. And Chosroes bade him rise from the ground, promising that he would grant all these things. So the ambassadors with the money came to Daras and the Persian army marched back.

Then indeed the fellow-ambassadors of Rufinus began to regard him with extreme suspicion themselves, and they also denounced him to the emperor, basing their judgment on the fact that Chosroes had been persuaded to concede him everything which he asked of him. However, the emperor showed him no disfavour on account of this. At a time not long after this Rufinus himself and Hermogenes were again sent to the court of Chosroes, and they immediately came to agreement with each other concerning the treaty, subject to the condition that both sides should give back all the places which each nation had wrested from the other in that war, and that there should no longer be any military post in Daras; as for the Iberians, it was agreed that the decision rested with them whether they should remain there in Byzantium or return to their own fatherland. And there were many who remained, and many also who returned to their ancestral homes. [532 A.D.] Thus, then, they concluded the so-called "endless peace," when the Emperor Justinian was already in the sixth year of his reign. And the Romans gave the Persians Pharangium and the fortress of Bolum together with the money, and the Persians gave the Romans the strongholds of Lazica. The Persians also returned Dagaris to the Romans, and received in return for him another man of no mean station. This Dagaris in later times often conquered the Huns in battle when they had invaded the land of the Romans, and drove them out; for he was an exceptionally able warrior. Thus both sides in the manner described made secure the treaty between them.

Straightway it came about that plots were formed against both rulers by their subjects; and I shall now explain how this happened. Chosroes, the son of Cabades, was a man of an unruly turn of mind and strangely fond of innovations. For this reason he himself was always full of excitement and alarms, and he was an unfailing cause of similar feelings in all others. All, therefore, who were men of action among the Persians, in vexation at his administration, were purposing to establish over themselves another king from the house of Cabades. And since they longed earnestly for the rule of Zames, which was made impossible by the law by reason of the disfigurement of his eye, as has been stated, they found upon consideration that the best course for them was to establish in power his child Cabades, who bore the same name as his grandfather, while Zames, as guardian of the child, should administer the affairs of the Persians as he wished. So they went to Zames and disclosed their plan, and, urging him on with great enthusiasm, they endeavoured to persuade him to undertake the thing. And since the plan pleased him, they were purposing to assail Chosroes at the fitting moment. But the plan was discovered and came to the knowledge of the king, and thus their proceedings were stopped. For Chosroes slew Zames himself and all his own brothers and those of Zames together with all their male offspring, and also all the Persian notables who had either begun or taken part in any way in the plot against him. Among these was Aspebedes, the brother of Chosroes' mother.

Cabades, however, the son of Zames, he was quite unable to kill; for he was still being reared under the chanaranges, Adergoudounbades. But he sent a message to the chanaranges, bidding him himself kill the boy he had reared; for he neither thought it well to shew mistrust, nor yet had he power to compel him. The chanaranges, therefore, upon hearing the commands of Chosroes, was exceedingly grieved and, lamenting the misfortune, he communicated to his wife and Cabades' nurse all that the king had commanded. Then the woman, bursting into tears and seizing the knees of her husband, entreated him by no means to kill Cabades. They therefore consulted together, and planned to bring up the child in the most secure concealment, and to send word in haste to Chosroes that Cabades had been put out of the world for him. And they sent word to the king to this effect, and concealed Cabades in such a way that the affair did not come to the notice of any one, except Varrames, their own child, and one of the servants who seemed to them to be in every way most trustworthy. But when, as time went on, Cabades came of age, the chanaranges began to fear lest what had been done should be brought to light; he therefore gave Cabades money and bade him depart and save himself by flight wherever he could. At that time, then, Chosroes and all the others were in ignorance of the fact that the chanaranges had carried this thing through.

At a later time Chosroes was making an invasion into the land of Colchis with a great army, as will be told in the following narrative[30]. And he was followed by the son of this same chanaranges, Varrames, who took with him a number of his servants, and among them the one who shared with him the knowledge of what had happened to Cabades; while there Varrames told the king everything regarding Cabades, and he brought forward the servant agreeing with him in every particular. When Chosroes learned this he was forthwith exceedingly angry, and he counted it a dreadful thing that he had suffered such things at the hand of a man who was his slave; and since he had no other means of getting the man under his hand he devised the following plan. When he was about to return homeward from the land of Colchis, he wrote to this chanaranges that he had decided to invade the land of the Romans with his whole army, not, however, by a single inroad into the country, but making two divisions of the Persian army, in order that the attack might be made upon the enemy on both sides of the River Euphrates. Now one division of the army he himself, as was natural, would lead into the hostile land, while to no one else of his subjects would he grant the privilege of holding equal honour with the king in this matter, except to the chanaranges himself on account of his valour. It was necessary, therefore, that the chanaranges should come speedily to meet him as he returned, in order that he might confer with him and give him all the directions which would be of advantage to the army, and that he should bid his attendants travel behind him on the road. When the chanaranges received this message, he was overjoyed at the honour shown him by the king, and in complete ignorance of his own evil plight, he immediately carried out the instructions. But in the course of this journey, since he was quite unable to sustain the toil of it (for he was a very old man), he relaxed his hold on the reins and fell off his horse, breaking the bone in his leg. It was therefore necessary for him to remain there quietly and be cared for, and the king came to that place and saw him. And Chosroes said to him that with his leg in such a plight it was not possible that he make the expedition with them, but that he must go to one of the fortresses in that region and receive treatment there from the physicians. Thus then Chosroes sent the man away on the road to death, and behind him followed the very men who were to destroy him in the fortress, a man who was in fact as well as in name an invincible general among the Persians, who had marched against twelve nations of barbarians and subjected them all to King Cabades. After Adergoudounbades had been removed from the world, Varrames, his son, received the office of chanaranges. Not long after this either Cabades himself, the son of Zames, or someone else who was assuming the name of Cabades came to Byzantium; certainly he resembled very closely in appearance Cabades, the king. And the Emperor Justinian, though in doubt concerning him, received him with great friendliness and honoured him as the grandson of Cabades. So then fared the Persians who rose against Chosroes.

Later on Chosroes destroyed also Mebodes for the following reason. While the king was arranging a certain important matter, he directed Zaberganes who was present to call Mebodes. Now it happened that Zaberganes was on hostile terms with Mebodes. When he came to him, he found him marshalling the soldiers under his command, and he said that the king summoned him to come as quickly as possible. And Mebodes promised that he would follow directly as soon as he should have arranged the matter in hand; but Zaberganes, moved by his hostility to him, reported to Chosroes that Mebodes did not wish to come at present, claiming to have some business or other. Chosroes, therefore, moved with anger, sent one of his attendants commanding Mebodes to go to the tripod. Now as to what this is I shall explain forthwith. An iron tripod stands always before the palace; and whenever anyone of the Persians learns that the king is angry with him, it is not right for such a man to flee for refuge to a sanctuary nor to go elsewhere, but he must seat himself by this tripod and await the verdict of the king, while no one at all dares protect him. There Mebodes sat in pitiable plight for many days, until he was seized and put to death at the command of Chosroes. Such was the final outcome of his good deeds to Chosroes.

XXIV

[Jan. 1, 532] At this same time an insurrection broke out unexpectedly in Byzantium among the populace, and, contrary to expectation, it proved to be a very serious affair, and ended in great harm to the people and to the senate, as the following account will shew. In every city the population has been divided for a long time past into the Blue and the Green factions; but within comparatively recent times it has come about that, for the sake of these names and the seats which the rival factions occupy in watching the games, they spend their money and abandon their bodies to the most cruel tortures, and even do not think it unworthy to die a most shameful death. And they fight against their opponents knowing not for what end they imperil themselves, but knowing well that, even if they overcome their enemy in the fight, the conclusion of the matter for them will be to be carried off straightway to the prison, and finally, after suffering extreme torture, to be destroyed. So there grows up in them against their fellow men a hostility which has no cause, and at no time does it cease or disappear, for it gives place neither to the ties of marriage nor of relationship nor of friendship, and the case is the same even though those who differ with respect to these colours be brothers or any other kin. They care neither for things divine nor human in comparison with conquering in these struggles; and it matters not whether a sacrilege is committed by anyone at all against God, or whether the laws and the constitution are violated by friend or by foe; nay even when they are perhaps ill supplied with the necessities of life, and when their fatherland is in the most pressing need and suffering unjustly, they pay no heed if only it is likely to go well with their "faction"; for so they name the bands of partisans. And even women join with them in this unholy strife, and they not only follow the men, but even resist them if opportunity offers, although they neither go to the public exhibitions at all, nor are they impelled by any other cause; so that I, for my part, am unable to call this anything except a disease of the soul. This, then, is pretty well how matters stand among the people of each and every city.

But at this time the officers of the city administration in Byzantium were leading away to death some of the rioters. But the members of the two factions, conspiring together and declaring a truce with each other, seized the prisoners and then straightway entered the prison and released all those who were in confinement there, whether they had been condemned on a charge of stirring up sedition, or for any other unlawful act. And all the attendants in the service of the city government were killed indiscriminately; meanwhile, all of the citizens who were sane-minded were fleeing to the opposite mainland, and fire was applied to the city as if it had fallen under the hand of an enemy. The sanctuary of Sophia and the baths of Zeuxippus, and the portion of the imperial residence from the propylaea as far as the so-called House of Ares were destroyed by fire, and besides these both the great colonnades which extended as far as the market place which bears the name of Constantine, in addition to many houses of wealthy men and a vast amount of treasure. During this time the emperor and his consort with a few members of the senate shut themselves up in the palace and remained quietly there. Now the watch-word which the populace passed around to one another was Nika[31], and the insurrection has been called by this name up to the present time.

The praetorian prefect at that time was John the Cappadocian, and Tribunianus, a Pamphylian by birth, was counsellor to the emperor; this person the Romans call "quaestor." One of these two men, John, was entirely without the advantages of a liberal education; for he learned nothing while attending the elementary school except his letters, and these, too, poorly enough; but by his natural ability he became the most powerful man of whom we know. For he was most capable in deciding upon what was needful and in finding a solution for difficulties. But he became the basest of all men and employed his natural power to further his low designs; neither consideration for God nor any shame before man entered into his mind, but to destroy the lives of many men for the sake of gain and to wreck whole cities was his constant concern. So within a short time indeed he had acquired vast sums of money, and he flung himself completely into the sordid life of a drunken scoundrel; for up to the time of lunch each day he would plunder the property of his subjects, and for the rest of the day occupy himself with drinking and with wanton deeds of lust. And he was utterly unable to control himself, for he ate food until he vomited, and he was always ready to steal money and more ready to bring it out and spend it. Such a man then was John. Tribunianus, on the other hand, both possessed natural ability and in educational attainments was inferior to none of his contemporaries; but he was extraordinarily fond of the pursuit of money and always ready to sell justice for gain; therefore every day, as a rule, he was repealing some laws and proposing others, selling off to those who requested it either favour according to their need.

Now as long as the people were waging this war with each other in behalf of the names of the colours, no attention was paid to the offences of these men against the constitution; but when the factions came to a mutual understanding, as has been said, and so began the sedition, then openly throughout the whole city they began to abuse the two and went about seeking them to kill. Accordingly the emperor, wishing to win the people to his side, instantly dismissed both these men from office. And Phocas, a patrician, he appointed praetorian prefect, a man of the greatest discretion and fitted by nature to be a guardian of justice; Basilides he commanded to fill the office of quaestor, a man known among the patricians for his agreeable qualities and a notable besides.

However, the insurrection continued no less violently under them. Now on the fifth day of the insurrection in the late afternoon the Emperor Justinian gave orders to Hypatius and Pompeius, nephews of the late emperor, Anastasius, to go home as quickly as possible, either because he suspected that some plot was being matured by them against his own person, or, it may be, because destiny brought them to this. But they feared that the people would force them to the throne (as in fact fell out), and they said that they would be doing wrong if they should abandon their sovereign when he found himself in such danger. When the Emperor Justinian heard this, he inclined still more to his suspicion, and he bade them quit the palace instantly. Thus, then, these two men betook themselves to their homes, and, as long as it was night, they remained there quietly.

But on the following day at sunrise it became known to the people that both men had quit the palace where they had been staying. So the whole population ran to them, and they declared Hypatius emperor and prepared to lead him to the market-place to assume the power. But the wife of Hypatius, Mary, a discreet woman, who had the greatest reputation for prudence, laid hold of her husband and would not let go, but cried out with loud lamentation and with entreaties to all her kinsmen that the people were leading him on the road to death. But since the throng overpowered her, she unwillingly released her husband, and he by no will of his own came to the Forum of Constantine, where they summoned him to the throne; then since they had neither diadem nor anything else with which it is customary for a king to be clothed, they placed a golden necklace upon his head and proclaimed him Emperor of the Romans. By this time the members of the senate were assembling, as many of them as had not been left in the emperor's residence, and many expressed the opinion that they should go to the palace to fight. But Origenes, a man of the senate, came forward and spoke as follows: "Fellow Romans, it is impossible that the situation which is upon us be solved in any way except by war. Now war and royal power are agreed to be the greatest of all things in the world. But when action involves great issues, it refuses to be brought to a successful conclusion by the brief crisis of a moment, but this is accomplished only by wisdom of thought and energy of action, which men display for a length of time. Therefore if we should go out against the enemy, our cause will hang in the balance, and we shall be taking a risk which will decide everything in a brief space of time; and, as regards the consequences of such action, we shall either fall down and worship Fortune or reproach her altogether. For those things whose issue is most quickly decided, fall, as a rule, under the sway of fortune. But if we handle the present situation more deliberately, not even if we wish shall we be able to take Justinian in the palace, but he will very speedily be thankful if he is allowed to flee; for authority which is ignored always loses its power, since its strength ebbs away with each day. Moreover we have other palaces, both Placillianae and the palace named from Helen, which this emperor should make his headquarters and from there he should carry on the war and attend to the ordering of all other matters in the best possible way." So spoke Origenes. But the rest, as a crowd is accustomed to do, insisted more excitedly and thought that the present moment was opportune, and not least of all Hypatius (for it was fated that evil should befall him) bade them lead the way to the hippodrome. But some say that he came there purposely, being well-disposed toward the emperor.

Now the emperor and his court were deliberating as to whether it would be better for them if they remained or if they took to flight in the ships. And many opinions were expressed favouring either course. And the Empress Theodora also spoke to the following effect: "As to the belief that a woman ought not to be daring among men or to assert herself boldly among those who are holding back from fear, I consider that the present crisis most certainly does not permit us to discuss whether the matter should be regarded in this or in some other way. For in the case of those whose interests have come into the greatest danger nothing else seems best except to settle the issue immediately before them in the best possible way. My opinion then is that the present time, above all others, is inopportune for flight, even though it bring safety. For while it is impossible for a man who has seen the light not also to die, for one who has been an emperor it is unendurable to be a fugitive. May I never be separated from this purple, and may I not live that day on which those who meet me shall not address me as mistress. If, now, it is your wish to save yourself, O Emperor, there is no difficulty. For we have much money, and there is the sea, here the boats. However consider whether it will not come about after you have been saved that you would gladly exchange that safety for death. For as for myself, I approve a certain ancient saying that royalty is a good burial-shroud." When the queen had spoken thus, all were filled with boldness, and, turning their thoughts towards resistance, they began to consider how they might be able to defend themselves if any hostile force should come against them. Now the soldiers as a body, including those who were stationed about the emperor's court, were neither well disposed to the emperor nor willing openly to take an active part in fighting, but were waiting for what the future would bring forth. All the hopes of the emperor were centred upon Belisarius and Mundus, of whom the former, Belisarius, had recently returned from the Persian war bringing with him a following which was both powerful and imposing, and in particular he had a great number of spearmen and guards who had received their training in battles and the perils of warfare. Mundus had been appointed general of the Illyrians, and by mere chance had happened to come under summons to Byzantium on some necessary errand, bringing with him Erulian barbarians.

When Hypatius reached the hippodrome, he went up immediately to where the emperor is accustomed to take his place and seated himself on the royal throne from which the emperor was always accustomed to view the equestrian and athletic contests. And from the palace Mundus went out through the gate which, from the circling descent, has been given the name of the Snail. Belisarius meanwhile began at first to go straight up toward Hypatius himself and the royal throne, and when he came to the adjoining structure where there has been a guard of soldiers from of old, he cried out to the soldiers commanding them to open the door for him as quickly as possible, in order that he might go against the tyrant. But since the soldiers had decided to support neither side, until one of them should be manifestly victorious, they pretended not to hear at all and thus put him off. So Belisarius returned to the emperor and declared that the day was lost for them, for the soldiers who guarded the palace were rebelling against him. The emperor therefore commanded him to go to the so-called Bronze Gate and the propylaea there. So Belisarius, with difficulty and not without danger and great exertion, made his way over ground covered by ruins and half-burned buildings, and ascended to the stadium. And when he had reached the Blue Colonnade which is on the right of the emperor's throne, he purposed to go against Hypatius himself first; but since there was a small door there which had been closed and was guarded by the soldiers of Hypatius who were inside, he feared lest while he was struggling in the narrow space the populace should fall upon him, and after destroying both himself and all his followers, should proceed with less trouble and difficulty against the emperor. Concluding, therefore, that he must go against the populace who had taken their stand in the hippodrome, a vast multitude crowding each other in great disorder, he drew his sword from its sheath and, commanding the others to do likewise, with a shout he advanced upon them at a run. But the populace, who were standing in a mass and not in order, at the sight of armoured soldiers who had a great reputation for bravery and experience in war, and seeing that they struck out with their swords unsparingly, beat a hasty retreat. Then a great outcry arose, as was natural, and Mundus, who was standing not far away, was eager to join in the fight, for he was a daring and energetic fellow but he was at a loss as to what he should do under the circumstances; when, however, he observed that Belisarius was in the struggle, he straightway made a sally into the hippodrome through the entrance which they call the Gate of Death. Then indeed from both sides the partisans of Hypatius were assailed with might and main and destroyed. When the rout had become complete and there had already been great slaughter of the populace, Boraedes and Justus, nephews of the Emperor Justinian, without anyone daring to lift a hand against them, dragged Hypatius down from the throne, and, leading him in, handed him over together with Pompeius to the emperor. And there perished among the populace on that day more than thirty thousand. But the emperor commanded the two prisoners to be kept in severe confinement. Then, while Pompeius was weeping and uttering pitiable words (for the man was wholly inexperienced in such misfortunes), Hypatius reproached him at length and said that those who were about to die unjustly should not lament. For in the beginning they had been forced by the people against their will, and afterwards they had come to the hippodrome with no thought of harming the emperor. And the soldiers killed both of them on the following day and threw their bodies into the sea. The emperor confiscated all their property for the public treasury, and also that of all the other members of the senate who had sided with them. Later, however, he restored to the children of Hypatius and Pompeius and to all others the titles which they had formerly held, and as much of their property as he had not happened to bestow upon his friends. This was the end of the insurrection in Byzantium.

XXV

Tribunianus and John were thus deprived of office, but at a later time they were both restored to the same positions. And Tribunianus lived on in office many years and died of disease, suffering no further harm from anyone. For he was a smooth fellow and agreeable in every way and well able by the excellence of his education to throw into the shade his affliction of avarice. But John was oppressive and severe alike with all men, inflicting blows upon those whom he met and plundering without respect absolutely all their money; consequently in the tenth year of his office he rightly and justly atoned for his lawless conduct in the following manner.

The Empress Theodora hated him above all others. And while he gave offence to the woman by the wrongs he committed, he was not of a mind to win her by flattery or by kindness in any way, but he openly set himself in opposition to her and kept slandering her to the emperor, neither blushing before her high station nor feeling shame because of the extraordinary love which the emperor felt for her. When the queen perceived what was being done, she purposed to slay the man, but in no way could she do this, since the Emperor Justinian set great store by him. And when John learned of the purpose of the queen regarding him, he was greatly terrified. And whenever he went into his chamber to sleep, he expected every night that some one of the barbarians would fall upon him to slay him; and he kept peeping out of the room and looking about the entrances and remained sleepless, although he had attached to himself many thousands of spearmen and guards, a thing which had been granted to no prefect before that time. But at daybreak, forgetting all his fears of things divine and human, he would become again a plague to all the Romans both in public and in private. And he conversed commonly with sorcerers, and constantly listened to profane oracles which portended for him the imperial office, so that he was plainly walking on air and lifted up by his hopes of the royal power. But in his rascality and the lawlessness of his conduct there was no moderation or abatement. And there was in him absolutely no regard for God, and even when he went to a sanctuary to pray and to pass the night, he did not do at all as the Christians are wont to do, but he clothed himself in a coarse garment appropriate to a priest of the old faith which they are now accustomed to call Hellenic, and throughout that whole night mumbled out some unholy words which he had practised, praying that the mind of the emperor might be still more under his control, and that he himself might be free from harm at the hands of all men.

At this time Belisarius, after subjugating Italy, came to Byzantium at the summons of the emperor with his wife Antonina, in order to march against the Persians[32]. And while in the eyes of all others he was an honoured and distinguished person, as was natural, John alone was hostile to him and worked actively against him, for no other reason than that he drew the hatred of all to himself, while Belisarius enjoyed an unequalled popularity. And it was on him that the hope of the Romans centred as he marched once more against the Persians, leaving his wife in Byzantium. Now Antonina, the wife of Belisarius, (for she was the most capable person in the world to contrive the impossible,) purposing to do a favour to the empress, devised the following plan. John had a daughter,

Euphemia, who had a great reputation for discretion, but a very young woman and for this reason very susceptible; this girl was exceedingly loved by her father, for she was his only child. By treating this young woman kindly for several days Antonina succeeded most completely in winning her friendship, and she did not refuse to share her secrets with her. And on one occasion when she was present alone with her in her room she pretended to lament the fate which was upon her, saying that although Belisarius had made the Roman empire broader by a goodly measure than it had been before, and though he had brought two captive kings and so great an amount of wealth to Byzantium, he found Justinian ungrateful; and in other respects she slandered the government as not just. Now Euphemia was overjoyed by these words, for she too was hostile to the present administration by reason of her fear of the empress, and she said: "And yet, dearest friend, it is you and Belisarius who are to blame for this, seeing that, though you have opportunity, you are not willing to use your power." And Antonina replied quickly: "It is because we are not able, my daughter, to undertake revolutions in camp, unless some of those here at home join with us in the task. Now if your father were willing, we should most easily organize this project and accomplish whatever God wills." When Euphemia heard this, she promised eagerly that the suggestion would be carried out, and departing from there she immediately brought the matter before her father. And he was pleased by the message (for he inferred that this undertaking offered him a way to the fulfilment of his prophecies and to the royal power), and straightway without any hesitation he assented, and bade his child arrange that on the following day he himself should come to confer with Antonina and give pledges. When Antonina learned the mind of John, she wished to lead him as far as possible astray from the understanding of the truth, so she said that for the present it was inadvisable that he should meet her, for fear lest some suspicion should arise strong enough to prevent proceedings; but she was intending straightway to depart for the East to join Belisarius. When, therefore, she had quit Byzantium and had reached the suburb (the one called Rufinianae which was the private possession of Belisarius), there John should come as if to salute her and to escort her forth on the journey, and they should confer regarding matters of state and give and receive their pledges. In saying this she seemed to John to speak well, and a certain day was appointed to carry out the plan. And the empress, hearing the whole account from Antonina, expressed approval of what she had planned, and by her exhortations raised her enthusiasm to a much higher pitch still.

When the appointed day was at hand, Antonina bade the empress farewell and departed from the city, and she went to Rufinianae, as if to begin on the following day her journey to the East; hither too came John at night in order to carry out the plan which had been agreed upon. Meanwhile the empress denounced to her husband the things which were being done by John to secure the tyranny, and she sent Narses, the eunuch, and Marcellus, the commander of the palace guards to Rufinianae with numerous soldiers, in order that they might investigate what was going on, and, if they found John setting about a revolution, that they might kill the man forthwith and return. So these departed for this task. But they say that the emperor got information of what was being done and sent one of John's friends to him forbidding him on any condition to meet Antonina secretly. But John (since it was fated that he should fare ill), disregarding the emperor's warning, about midnight met Antonina, close by a certain wall behind which she had stationed Narses and Marcellus with their men that they might hear what was said. There, while John with unguarded tongue was assenting to the plans for the attack and binding himself with the most dread oaths, Narses and Marcellus suddenly set upon him. But in the natural confusion which resulted the body-guards of John (for they stood close by) came immediately to his side. And one of them smote Marcellus with his sword, not knowing who he was, and thus John was enabled to escape with them, and reached the city with all speed. And if he had had the courage to go straightway before the emperor, I believe that he would have suffered no harm at his hand; but as it was, he fled for refuge to the sanctuary, and gave the empress opportunity to work her will against him at her pleasure.

[May, 541] Thus, then, from being prefect he became a private citizen, and rising from that sanctuary he was conveyed to another, which is situated in the suburb of the city of Cyzicus called by the Cyzicenes Artace. There he donned the garb of a priest, much against his will, not a bishop's gown however, but that of a presbyter, as they are called. But he was quite unwilling to perform the office of a priest lest at some time it should be a hindrance to his entering again into office; for he was by no means ready to relinquish his hopes. All his property was immediately confiscated to the public treasury, but a large proportion of this the emperor remitted to him, for he was still inclined to spare him. There it was possible for John to live, disregarding all dangers and enjoying great wealth, both that which he himself had concealed and that which by the decision of the emperor remained with him, and to indulge in luxury at his pleasure, and, if he had reasoned wisely, to consider his present lot a happy one. For this reason all the Romans were exceedingly vexed with the man, because, forsooth, after proving himself the basest of all demons, contrary to his deserts he was leading a life happier than before. But God, I think, did not suffer John's retribution to end thus, but prepared for him a greater punishment. And it fell out thus.

There was in Cyzicus a certain bishop named Eusebius, a man harsh to all who came in his way, and no less so than John; this man the Cyzicenes denounced to the emperor and summoned to justice. And since they accomplished nothing inasmuch as Eusebius circumvented them by his great power, certain youths agreed together and killed him in the market-place of Cyzicus. Now it happened that John had become especially hostile to Eusebius, and hence the suspicion of the plot fell upon him. Accordingly men were sent from the senate to investigate this act of pollution. And these men first confined John in a prison, and then this man who had been such a powerful prefect, and had been inscribed among the patricians and had mounted the seat of the consuls, than which nothing seems greater, at least in the Roman state, they made to stand naked like any robber or footpad, and thrashing him with many blows upon his back, compelled him to tell his past life. And while John had not been clearly convicted as guilty of the murder of Eusebius, it seemed that God's justice was exacting from him the penalties of the world. Thereafter they stripped him of all his goods and put him naked on board a ship, being wrapped in a single cloak, and that a very rough one purchased for some few obols; and wherever the ship anchored, those who had him in charge commanded him to ask from those he met bread or obols. Thus begging everywhere along the way he was conveyed to the city of Antinous in Aegypt. And this is now the third year during which they have been guarding him there in confinement. As for John himself, although he has fallen into such troubles, he has not relinquished his hope of royal power, but he made up his mind to denounce certain Alexandrians as owing money to the public treasury. Thus then John the Cappadocian ten years afterward was overtaken by this punishment for his political career.

XXVI

At that time the Emperor again designated Belisarius General of the East, and, sending him to Libya, gained over the country, as will be told later on in my narrative. When this information came to Chosroes and the Persians, they were mightily vexed, and they already repented having made peace with the Romans, because they perceived that their power was extending greatly. And Chosroes sent envoys to Byzantium, and said that he rejoiced with the Emperor Justinian, and he asked with a laugh to receive his share of the spoils from Libya, on the ground that the emperor would never have been able to conquer in the war with the Vandals if the Persians had not been at peace with him. So then Justinian made a present of money to Chosroes, and not long afterwards dismissed the envoys.

In the city of Daras the following event took place. There was a certain John there serving in a detachment of infantry; this man, in conspiracy with some few of the soldiers, but not all, took possession of the city, essaying to make himself tyrant. Then he established himself in a palace as if in a citadel, and was strengthening his tyranny every day. And if it had not happened that the Persians were continuing to keep peace with the Romans, irreparable harm would have come from this affair to the Romans. But as it was, this was prevented by the agreement which had already been reached, as I have said. On the fourth day of the tyranny some soldiers conspired together, and by the advice of Mamas, the priest of the city, and Anastasius, one of the notable citizens, they went up to the palace at high noon, each man hiding a small sword under his garment. And first at the door of the courtyard they found some few of the body-guards, whom they slew immediately. Then they entered the men's apartment and laid hold upon the tyrant; but some say that the soldiers were not the first to do this, but that while they were still hesitating in the courtyard and trembling at the danger, a certain sausage-vendor who was with them rushed in with his cleaver and meeting John smote him unexpectedly. But the blow which had been dealt him was not a fatal one, this account goes on to say, and he fled with a great outcry and suddenly fell among these very soldiers. Thus they laid hands upon the man and immediately set fire to the palace and burned it, in order that there might be left no hope from there for those making revolutions; and John they led away to the prison and bound. And one of them, fearing lest the soldiers, upon learning that the tyrant survived, might again make trouble for the city, killed John, and in this way stopped the confusion. Such, then, was the progress of events touching this tyranny.

FOOTNOTES
[1] Cf. Iliad xi. 385 [Greek: toxota, lôbêtêr, kerai aglae, parthenopipa], the only place where [Greek: toxotês] occurs in Homer.

[2] Cf. Iliad v. 192.

[3] Cf. Iliad viii. 267; xi. 371.

[4] Cf. Iliad iv. 113.

[5] Cf. Iliad iv. 123.

[6] Cf. Iliad xi. 390.

[7] The trench crossed the plain in an approximately straight line. The army of the Ephthalitae were drawn up behind it, facing the advancing Persians, while a few of them went out beyond the trench to draw the attack of the Persians.

[8] Cf. Thuc. ii. 76, 4.

[9] Cf. Book VII. xxvi. 4.

[10] Cf. Thuc. i. 128.

[11] A division of no fixed number.

[12] Cf. Book I. ii. 15.

[13] Modern Erzeroum.

[14] i.e. "by force."

[15] Cf. Book VIII. xiii. 15.

[16] Cf. Iliad xxiv. 348; Odyssey x. 279.

[17] Lebanon.

[18] Roman formation.
a--a, trench.
1. Bouzes and Pharas.
2. Sunicas and Aigan.
3. John, Cyril, Marcellus, Germanus, and Dorotheus.
4. Simmas and Ascan.
5. Belisarius and Hermogenes.

[An illustration of a Roman formation.]

```
         1.                        3.
    (h)=======      |----|     ==========
      hill        2.--| 5. |--4.
       a_____|     |_____a
              ==================
```

[19] Cf. Book I. x. 2.

[20] Cf. Book I. xii. 21.

[21] Cf. Book I. xiii. 2.

[22] "Euphratesia"; cf. section 2.

[23] Title meaning a patrician. See Index.

[24] Ch. xiv. 28-54.

[25] The coast described here is that of Arabia.

[26] Rather the "Arabian Gulf."

[27] Cf. ch. xv. 31.

[28] In Latin serica, as coming from the Chinese (Seres).

[29] Cf. chap. xvi. 7.

[30] Cf. Book II. xvii.

[31] i.e. "Conquer."

[32] Book VI. xxx. 30.

Book II: The Persian War (Part II)

I

Not long after this Chosroes, upon learning that Belisarius had begun to win Italy also for the Emperor Justinian, was no longer able to restrain his thoughts but he wished to discover pretexts, in order that he might break the treaty on some grounds which would seem plausible. And he conferred with Alamoundaras concerning this matter and commanded him to provide causes for war. So Alamoundaras brought against Arethas, the charge that he, Arethas, was doing him violence in a matter of boundary lines, and he entered into conflict with him in time of peace, and began to overrun the land of the Romans on this pretext. And he declared that, as for him, he was not breaking the treaty between the Persians and Romans, for neither one of them had included him in it. And this was true. For no mention of Saracens was ever made in treaties, on the ground that they were included under the names of Persians and Romans. Now this country which at that time was claimed by both tribes of Saracens[1] is called Strata, and extends to the south of the city of Palmyra; nowhere does it produce a single tree or any of the useful growth of corn-lands, for it is burned exceedingly dry by the sun, but from of old it has been devoted to the pasturage of some few flocks. Now Arethas maintained that the place belonged to the Romans, proving his assertion by the name which has long been applied to it by all (for Strata signifies "a paved road" in the Latin tongue), and he also adduced the testimonies of men of the oldest times. Alamoundaras, however, was by no means inclined to quarrel concerning the name, but he claimed that tribute had been given him from of old for the pasturage there by the owners of the flocks. The Emperor Justinian therefore entrusted the settlement of the disputed points to Strategius; a patrician and administrator of the royal treasures, and besides a man of wisdom and of good ancestry, and with him Summus, who had commanded the troops in Palestine. This Summus was the brother of Julian, who not long before had served as envoy to the Aethiopians and Homeritae. And the one of them, Summus, insisted that the Romans ought not to surrender the country, but Strategius begged of the emperor that he should not do the Persians the favour of providing them with pretexts for the war which they already desired, for the sake of a small bit of land and one of absolutely no account, but altogether unproductive and unsuitable for crops. The Emperor Justinian, therefore, took the matter under consideration, and a long time was spent in the settlement of the question.

But Chosroes, the King of the Persians, claimed that the treaty had been broken by Justinian, who had lately displayed great opposition to his house, in that he had attempted in time of peace to attach Alamoundaras to himself. For, as he said, Summus, who had recently gone to the Saracen ostensibly to arrange matters, had hoodwinked him by promises of large sums of money on condition that he should join the Romans, and he brought forward a letter which, he alleged, the Emperor Justinian had written to Alamoundaras concerning these things. He also declared that he had sent a letter to some of the Huns, in which he urged them to invade the land of the Persians and to do extensive damage to the country thereabout. This letter he asserted to have been put into his hands by the Huns themselves who had come before him. So then Chosroes, with these charges against the Romans, was purposing to break off the treaty. But as to whether he was speaking the truth in these matters, I am not able to say.

II

At this point Vittigis, the leader of the Goths, already worsted in the war, sent two envoys to him to persuade him to march against the Romans; but the men whom he sent were not Goths, in order that the real character of the embassy might not be at once obvious and so make negotiations useless, but Ligurian priests who were attracted to this enterprise by rich gifts of money. One of these men, who seemed to be the more worthy, undertook the embassy assuming the pretended name of bishop which did not belong to him at all, while the other followed as his attendant. And when in the course of the journey they came to the land of Thrace, they attached to themselves a man from there to be an interpreter of the Syriac and the Greek tongues, and without being detected by any of the Romans, they reached the land of Persia. For inasmuch as they were at peace, they were not keeping a strict guard over that region. And coming before Chosroes they spoke as follows: "It is true, O King, that all other envoys undertake their task for the sake of advantages to themselves as a rule, but we have been sent by Vittigis, the king of the Goths and the Italians, in order to speak in behalf of thy kingdom; and consider that he is now present before thee speaking these words. If anyone should say, O King, putting all in a word, that thou hast given up thy kingdom and all men everywhere to Justinian, he would be speaking correctly. For since he is by nature a meddler and a lover of those things which in no way belong to him, and is not able to abide by the settled order of things, he has conceived the desire of seizing upon the whole earth, and has become eager to acquire for himself each and every state. Accordingly (since he was neither able alone to assail the Persians, nor with the Persians opposing him to proceed against the others), he decided to deceive thee with the pretence of peace, and by forcing the others to subjection to acquire mighty forces against thy state. Therefore, after having already destroyed the kingdom of the Vandals and subjugated the Moors, while the Goths because of their friendship stood aside for him, he has come against us bringing vast sums of money and many men. Now it is evident that, if he is able also to crush the Goths utterly, he will with us and those already enslaved march against the Persians, neither considering the name of friendship nor blushing before any of his sworn promises. While, therefore, some hope of safety is still left thee, do not do us any further wrong nor suffer it thyself, but see in our misfortunes what will a little later befall the Persians; and consider that the Romans could never be well-disposed to thy kingdom, and that when they become more powerful, they will not hesitate at all to display their enmity toward the Persians. Use, therefore, this good chance while the time fits, lest thou seek for it after it has ceased. For when once the time of opportunity has passed, it is not its nature to return again. And it is better by anticipating to be in security, than by delaying beyond the opportune time to suffer the most miserable fate possible at the hands of the enemy."

When Chosroes heard this, it seemed to him that Vittigis advised well, and he was still more eager to break off the treaty. For, moved as he was by envy toward the Emperor Justinian, he neglected completely to consider that the words were spoken to him by men who were bitter enemies of Justinian. But because he wished the thing he willingly consented to be persuaded. And he did the very same thing a little later in the case of the addresses of the Armenians and of the Lazi, which will be spoken of directly. And yet they were bringing as charges against Justinian the very things which would naturally be encomiums for a worthy monarch, namely that he was exerting himself to make his realm larger and much more splendid. For these accusations one might make also against Cyrus, the King of the Persians, and Alexander, the Macedonian. But justice is never accustomed to dwell together with envy. For these reasons, then, Chosroes was purposing to break off the treaty.

III

At this same time another event also occurred; it was as follows. That Symeon who had given Pharangium into the hands of the Romans persuaded the Emperor Justinian, while the war was still at its height, to present him with certain villages of Armenia. And becoming master of these places, he was plotted against and murdered by those who had formerly possessed them. After this crime had been committed, the perpetrators of the murder fled into the land of Persia. They were two brothers, sons of Perozes. And when the Emperor heard this, he gave over the villages to Amazaspes, the nephew of Symeon, and appointed him ruler over the Armenians. This Amazaspes, as time went on, was denounced to the Emperor Justinian by one of his friends, Acacius by name, on the ground that he was abusing the Armenians and wished to give over to the Persians Theodosiopolis and certain other fortresses. After telling this, Acacius, by the emperor's will, slew Amazaspes treacherously, and himself secured the command over the Armenians by the gift of the emperor. And being base by nature, he gained the opportunity of displaying his inward character, and he proved to be the most cruel of all men toward his subjects. For he plundered their property without excuse and ordained that they should pay an unheard-of tax of four centenaria[2]. But the Armenians, unable to bear him any longer, conspired together and slew Acacius and fled for refuge to Pharangium.

Therefore the emperor sent Sittas against them from Byzantium. For Sittas had been delaying there since the time when the treaty was made with the Persians. So he came to Armenia, but at first he entered upon the war reluctantly and exerted himself to calm the people and to restore the population to their former habitations, promising to persuade the emperor to remit to them the payment of the new tax. But since the emperor kept assailing him with frequent reproaches for his hesitation, led on by the slanders of Adolius, the son of Acacius, Sittas at last made his preparations for the conflict. First of all he attempted by means of promises of many good things to win over some of the Armenians by persuasion and to attach them to his cause, in order that the task of overpowering the others might be attended with less difficulty and toil. And the tribe called the Aspetiani, great in power and in numbers, was willing to join him. And they went to Sittas and begged him to give them pledges in writing that, if they abandoned their kinsmen in the battle and came to the Roman army, they should remain entirely free from harm, retaining their own possessions. Now Sittas was delighted and wrote to them in tablets, giving them pledges just as they desired of him; he then sealed the writing and sent it to them. Then, confident that by their help he would be victorious in the war without fighting, he went with his whole army to a place called Oenochalakon, where the Armenians had their camp. But by some chance those who carried the tablets went by another road and did not succeed at all in meeting the Aspetiani. Moreover a portion of the Roman army happened upon some few of them, and not knowing the agreement which had been made, treated them as enemies. And Sittas himself caught some of their women and children in a cave and slew them, either because he did not understand what had happened or because he was angry with the Aspetiani for not joining him as had been agreed.

But they, being now possessed with anger, arrayed themselves for battle with all the rest. But since both armies were on exceedingly difficult ground where precipices abounded, they did not fight in one place, but scattered about among the ridges and ravines. So it happened that some few of the Armenians and Sittas with not many of his followers came close upon each other, with only a ravine lying between them. Both parties were horsemen. Then Sittas with a few men following him crossed the ravine and advanced against the enemy; the Armenians, after withdrawing to the rear, stopped, and Sittas pursued no further but remained where he was. Suddenly someone from the Roman army, an Erulian by birth, who had been pursuing the enemy, returning impetuously from them came up to Sittas and his men. Now as it happened Sittas had planted his spear in the ground; and the Erulian's horse fell upon this with a great rush and shattered it. And the general was exceedingly annoyed by this, and one of the Armenians, seeing him, recognized him and declared to all the others that it was Sittas. For it happened that he had no helmet on his head. Thus it did not escape the enemy that he had come there with only a few men. Sittas, then, upon hearing the Armenian say this, since his spear, as has been said, lay broken in two on the ground, drew his sword and attempted immediately to recross the ravine. But the enemy advanced upon him with great eagerness, and a soldier overtaking him in the ravine struck him a glancing blow with his sword on the top of his head; and he took off the whole scalp, but the steel did not injure the bone at all. And Sittas continued to press forward still more than before, but Artabanes, son of John of the Arsacidae, fell upon him from behind and with a thrust of his spear killed him. Thus Sittas was removed from the world after no notable fashion, in a manner unworthy of his valour and his continual achievements against the enemy, a man who was extremely handsome in appearance and a capable warrior, and a general second to none of his contemporaries. But some say that Sittas did not die at the hand of Artabanes, but that Solomon, a very insignificant man among the Armenians, destroyed him.

After the death of Sittas the emperor commanded Bouzes to go against the Armenians; and he, upon drawing near, sent to them promising to effect a reconciliation between the emperor and all the Armenians, and asking that some of their notables should come to confer with him on these matters. Now the Armenians as a whole were unable to trust Bouzes nor were they willing to receive his proposals. But there was a certain man of the Arsacidae who was especially friendly with him, John by name, the father of Artabanes, and this man, trusting in Bouzes as his friend came to him with his son-in-law, Bassaces, and a few others; but when these men had reached the spot where they were to meet Bouzes on the following day, and had made their bivouac there, they perceived that they had come into a place surrounded by the Roman army. Bassaces, the son-in-law, therefore earnestly entreated John to fly. And since he was not able to persuade him, he left him there alone, and in company with all the others eluded the Romans, and went back again by the same road. And Bouzes found John alone and slew him; and since after this the Armenians had no hope of ever reaching an agreement with the Romans, and since they were unable to prevail over the emperor in war, they came before the Persian king led by Bassaces, an energetic man. And the leading men among them came at that time into the presence of Chosroes and spoke as follows: "Many of us, O Master, are Arsacidae, descendants of that Arsaces who was not unrelated to the Parthian kings when the Persian realm lay under the hand of the Parthians, and who proved himself an illustrious king, inferior to none of his time. Now we have come to thee, and all of us have become slaves and fugitives, not, however, of our own will, but under most hard constraint, as it might seem by reason of the Roman power, but in truth, O King, by reason of thy decision, if, indeed, he who gives the strength to those who wish to do injustice should himself justly bear also the blame of their misdeeds. Now we shall begin our account from a little distance back in order that you may be able to follow the whole course of events. Arsaces, the last king of our ancestors, abdicated his throne willingly in favour of Theodosius, the Roman Emperor, on condition that all who should belong to his family through all time should live unhampered in every respect, and in particular should in no case be subject to taxation. And we have preserved the agreement, until you, the Persians, made this much-vaunted treaty, which, as we think, one would not err in calling a sort of common destruction. For from that time, disregarding friend and foe, he who is in name thy friend, O King, but in fact thy enemy, has turned everything in the world upside down and wrought complete confusion. And this thou thyself shalt know at no distant time, as soon as he is able to subdue completely the people of the West. For what thing which was before forbidden has he not done? or what thing which was well established has he not disturbed? Did he not ordain for us the payment of a tax which did not exist before, and has he not enslaved our neighbours, the Tzani, who were autonomous, and has he not set over the king of the wretched Lazi a Roman magistrate? an act neither in keeping with the natural order of things nor very easy to explain in words. Has he not sent generals to the men of Bosporus, the subjects of the Huns, and attached to himself the city which in no way belongs to him, and has he not made a defensive alliance with the Aethiopian kingdoms, of which the Romans had never even heard? More than this he has made the Homeritae his possession and the Red Sea, and he is adding the Palm Groves to the Roman dominion. We omit to speak of the fate of the Libyans and of the Italians. The whole earth is not large enough for the man; it is too small a thing for him to conquer all the world together. But he is even looking about the heavens and is searching the retreats beyond the ocean, wishing to gain for himself some other world. Why, therefore, O King, dost thou still delay? Why dost thou respect that most accursed peace, in order forsooth that he may make thee the last morsel of all? If it is thy wish to learn what kind of a man Justinian would shew himself toward those who yield to him, the example is to be sought near at hand from ourselves and from the wretched Lazi; and if thou wishest to see how he is accustomed to treat those who are unknown to him and who have done him not the least wrong, consider the Vandals and the Goths and the Moors. But the chief thing has not yet been spoken. Has he not made efforts in time of peace to win over by deception thy slave, Alamoundaras, O most mighty King, and to detach him from thy kingdom, and has he not striven recently to attach to himself the Huns who are utterly unknown to him, in order to make trouble for thee? And yet an act more strange than this has not been performed in all time. For since he perceived, as I think, that the overthrow of the western world would speedily be accomplished, he has already taken in hand to assail you of the East, since the Persian power alone has been left for him to grapple with. The peace, therefore, as far as concerns him, has already been broken for thee, and he himself has set an end to the endless peace. For they break the peace, not who may be first in arms, but they who may be caught plotting against their neighbours in time of peace. For the crime has been committed by him who attempts it, even though success be lacking. Now as for the course which the war will follow, this is surely clear to everyone. For it is not those who furnish causes for war, but those who defend themselves against those who furnish them, who are accustomed always to conquer their enemies. Nay more, the contest will not be evenly matched for us even in point of strength. For, as it happens, the majority of the Roman soldiers are at the end of the world, and as for the two generals who were the best they had, we come here having slain the one, Sittas, and Belisarius will never again be seen by Justinian. For disregarding his master, he has remained in the West, holding the power of Italy himself. So that when thou goest against the enemy, no one at all will confront thee, and thou wilt have us leading the army with good will, as is natural, and with a thorough knowledge of the country." When Chosroes heard this he was pleased, and calling together all who were of noble blood among the Persians, he disclosed to all of them what Vittigis had written and what the Armenians had said, and laid before them the question as to what should be done. Then many opinions were expressed inclining to either side, but finally it was decided that they must open hostilities against the Romans at the beginning of spring. [539 A.D.] For it was the late autumn season, in the thirteenth year of the reign of the Emperor Justinian. The Romans, however, did not suspect this, nor did they think that the Persians would ever break the so-called endless peace, although they heard that Chosroes blamed their emperor for his successes in the West, and that he preferred against him the charges which I have lately mentioned.

IV

[539 A.D.] At that time also the comet appeared, at first about as long as a tall man, but later much larger. And the end of it was toward the west and its beginning toward the east, and it followed behind the sun itself. For the sun was in Capricorn and it was in Sagittarius. And some called it "the swordfish" because it was of goodly length and very sharp at the point, and others called it "the bearded star"; it was seen for more than forty days. Now those who were wise in these matters disagreed utterly with each other, and one announced that one thing, another that another thing was indicated by this star; but I only write what took place and I leave to each one to judge by the outcome as he wishes. Straightway a mighty Hunnic army crossing the Danube River fell as a scourge upon all Europe, a thing which had happened many times before, but which had never brought such a multitude of woes nor such dreadful ones to the people of that land. For from the Ionian Gulf these barbarians plundered everything in order as far as the suburbs of Byzantium. And they captured thirty-two fortresses in Illyricum, and they carried by storm the city of Cassandria (which the ancients called Potidaea, as far as we know), never having fought against walls before. And taking with them the money and leading away one hundred and twenty thousand captives, they all retired homeward without encountering any opposition. In later times too they often came there and brought upon the Romans irreparable calamity. This same people also assailed the wall of the Chersonesus, where they overpowered those who were defending themselves from the wall, and approaching through the surf of the sea, scaled the fortifications on the so-called Black Gulf; thus they got within the long wall, and falling unexpectedly upon the Romans in the Chersonesus they slew many of them and made prisoners of almost all the survivors. Some few of them also crossed the strait between Sestus and Abydus, and after plundering the Asiatic country, they returned again to the Chersonesus, and with the rest of the army and all the booty betook themselves to their homes. In another invasion they plundered Illyricum and Thessaly and attempted to storm the wall at Thermopylae; and since the guards on the walls defended them most valiantly, they sought out the ways around and unexpectedly found the path which leads up the mountain which rises there[3]. In this way they destroyed almost all the Greeks except the Peloponnesians, and then withdrew. And the Persians not long afterwards broke off the treaty and wrought such harm to the Romans of the East as I shall set forth immediately.

Belisarius, after humbling Vittigis, the king of the Goths and Italians, brought him alive to Byzantium. And I shall now proceed to tell how the army of the Persians invaded the land of the Romans. When the Emperor Justinian perceived that Chosroes was eager for war, he wished to offer him some counsel and to dissuade him from the undertaking. Now it happened that a certain man had come to Byzantium from the city of Daras, Anastasius by name, well known for his sagacity; he it was who had broken the tyranny which had been established recently in Daras. Justinian therefore wrote a letter and sent it by this Anastasius to Chosroes; and the message of the letter was as follows: "It is the part of men of discretion and those by whom divine things are treated with due respect, when causes of war arise, and in particular against men who are in the truest sense friends, to exert all their power to put an end to them; but it belongs to foolish men and those who most lightly bring on themselves the enmity of Heaven to devise occasions for war and insurrection which have no real existence. Now to destroy peace and enter upon war is not a difficult matter, since the nature of things is such as to make the basest activities easy for the most dishonourable men. But when they have brought about war according to their intention, to return again to peace is for men, I think, not easy. And yet thou chargest me with writing letters which were not written with any dark purpose, and thou hast now made haste to interpret these with arbitrary judgment, not in the sense in which we conceived them when we wrote them, but in a way which will be of advantage to thee in thy eagerness to carry out thy plans not without some pretext. But for us it is possible to point out that thy Alamoundaras recently overran our land and performed outrageous deeds in time of peace, to wit, the capture of towns, the seizure of property, the massacre and enslavement of such a multitude of men, concerning which it will be thy duty not to blame us, but to defend thyself. For the crimes of those who have done wrong are made manifest to their neighbours by their acts, not by their thoughts. But even with these things as they are, we have still decided to hold to peace, but we hear that thou in thy eagerness to make war upon the Romans art fabricating accusations which do not belong to us at all. Natural enough, this; for while those who are eager to preserve the present order of things repel even those charges against their friends which are most pressing, those who are not satisfied with established friendships exert themselves to provide even pretexts which do not exist. But this would not seem to be becoming even to ordinary men, much less to kings. But leaving aside these things do thou consider the number of those who will be destroyed on both sides in the course of the war, and consider well who will justly bear the blame for those things which will come to pass, and ponder upon the oaths which thou didst take when thou didst carry away the money, and consider that if, after that, thou wrongly dishonour them by some tricks or sophistries, thou wouldst not be able to pervert them; for Heaven is too mighty to be deceived by any man." When Chosroes saw this message, he neither made any immediate answer nor did he dismiss Anastasius, but he compelled him to remain there.

V

[540 A.D.] When the winter was already reaching its close, and the thirteenth year of the reign of the Emperor Justinian was ending, Chosroes, son of Cabades, invaded the land of the Romans at the opening of spring with a mighty army, and openly broke the so-called endless peace. But he did not enter by the country between the rivers, but advanced with the Euphrates on his right. On the other side of the river stands the last Roman stronghold which is called Circesium, an exceedingly strong place, since the River Aborras, a large stream, has its mouth at this point and mingles with the Euphrates, and this fortress lies exactly in the angle which is made by the junction of the two rivers. And a long second wall outside the fortress cuts off the land between the two rivers, and completes the form of a triangle around Circesium. Chosroes, therefore, not wishing to make trial of so strong a fortress and not having in mind to cross the River Euphrates, but rather to go against the Syrians and Cilicians, without any hesitation led his army forward, and after advancing for what, to an unencumbered traveller, is about a three-days' journey along the bank of the Euphrates, he came upon the city of Zenobia; this place Zenobia had built in former times, and, as was natural, she gave her name to the city. Now Zenobia was the wife of Odonathus, the ruler of the Saracens of that region, who had been on terms of peace with the Romans from of old. This Odonathus rescued for the Romans the Eastern Empire when it had come under the power of the Medes; but this took place in former times. Chosroes then came near to Zenobia, but upon learning that the place was not important and observing that the land was untenanted and destitute of all good things, he feared lest any time spent by him there would be wasted on an affair of no consequence and would be a hindrance to great undertakings, and he attempted to force the place to surrender. But meeting with no success, he hastened his march forward.

After again accomplishing a journey of equal extent, he reached the city of Sura, which is on the River Euphrates, and stopped very close to it. There it happened that the horse on which Chosroes was riding neighed and stamped the ground with his foot. And the Magi considered the meaning of this incident and announced that the place would be captured. Chosroes then made camp and led his army against the fortifications to assail the wall. Now it happened that a certain Arsaces, an Armenian by birth, was commander of the soldiers in the town; and he made the soldiers mount the parapets, and fighting from there most valiantly slew many of the enemy, but was himself struck by an arrow and died. And then, since it was late in the day, the Persians retired to their camp in order to assail the wall again on the following day; but the Romans were in despair since their leader was dead, and were purposing to make themselves suppliants of Chosroes. On the following day, therefore, they sent the bishop of the city to plead for them and to beg that the town be spared; so he took with him some of his attendants, who carried fowls and wine and clean loaves, and came before Chosroes; there he threw himself on the ground, and with tears supplicated him to spare a pitiable population and a city altogether without honour in the eyes of the Romans, and one which in past times had never been of any account to the Persians, and which never would be such thereafter; and he promised that the men of Sura would give him ransom worthy of themselves and the city which they inhabited. But Chosroes was angry with the townsmen because, being the first he had met of all the Romans, they had not willingly received him into their city, but even daring to raise their arms against him had slain a large number of Persian notables. However he did not disclose his anger, but carefully concealed it behind a smooth countenance, in order that by carrying out the punishment of the inhabitants of Sura he might make himself in the eyes of the Romans a fearful person and one not to be resisted. For by acting in this way he calculated that those who would from time to time come in his way would yield to him without trouble. Accordingly with great friendliness he caused the bishop to rise, and receiving the gifts, gave the impression, in a way, that he would immediately confer with the notables of the Persians concerning the ransom of the townsmen, and would settle their request favourably. Thus he dismissed the bishop and his following without any suspicion of the plot, and he sent with him certain of the men of note among the Persians, who were to be ostensibly an escort. These men he secretly commanded to go with him as far as the wall, encouraging him and cheering him with fair hopes, so that he and all those with him should be seen by those inside rejoicing and fearing nothing. But when the guards had set the gate open and were about to receive them into the city, they were to throw a stone or block of wood between the threshold and the gate and not allow them to shut it, but should themselves for a time stand in the way of those who wished to close it; for not long afterwards the army would follow them.

After giving these directions to the men Chosroes made ready the army, and commanded them to advance upon the city on the run whenever he should give the signal. So when they came close to the fortifications, the Persians bade farewell to the bishop and remained outside, and the townsmen, seeing that the man was exceedingly happy and that he was being escorted in great honour by the enemy, forgetting all their difficulties opened the gate wide, and received the priest and his following with clapping of hands and much shouting. And when all got inside, the guards began to push the gate in order to close it, but the Persians flung down a stone, which they had provided, between it and the threshold. And the guards pushed and struggled still more, but were quite unable to get the gate back to the threshold. On the other hand they dared not open it again, since they perceived that it was held by the enemy. But some say that it was not a stone but a block of wood which the Persians threw into the gateway. When the townsmen had as yet scarcely realized the plot, Chosroes was at hand with his whole army, and the barbarians forced back and flung open the gate, which was soon carried by storm. Straightway, then, Chosroes, filled with wrath, plundered the houses and put to death great numbers of the population; all the remainder he reduced to slavery, and setting fire to the whole city razed it to the ground. Then he dismissed Anastasius, bidding him announce to the Emperor Justinian where in the world he had left Chosroes, son of Cabades.

Afterwards either through motives of humanity or of avarice, or as granting a favour to a woman whom he had taken as a captive from the city, Euphemia by name, Chosroes decided to shew some kindness to the inhabitants of Sura; for he had conceived for this woman an extraordinary love (for she was exceedingly beautiful to look upon), and had made her his wedded wife. He sent, accordingly, to Sergiopolis, a city subject to the Romans, named from Sergius, a famous saint, distant from the captured city one hundred and twenty-six stades and lying to the south of it in the so-called Barbarian Plain, and bade Candidus, the bishop of the city, purchase the captives, twelve thousand in number, for two centenaria. But the bishop, alleging that he had no money, refused absolutely to undertake the matter. Chosroes therefore requested him to set down in a document the agreement that he would give the money at a later time, and thus to purchase for a small sum such a multitude of slaves. Candidus did as directed, promising to give the money within a year, and swore the most dire oaths, specifying that he should receive the following punishment if he should not give the money at the time agreed upon, that he should pay double the amount and should himself be no longer a priest, as one who had neglected his sworn promise. And after setting down these things in writing, Candidus received all the inhabitants of Sura. And some few among them survived, but the majority, unable to support the misery which had fallen to their lot, succumbed soon afterwards. After the settlement of this affair Chosroes led his army forward.

VI

It had happened a little before this that the emperor had divided into two parts the military command of the East, leaving the portion as far as the River Euphrates under the control of

Belisarius who formerly held the command of the whole, while the portion from there as far as the Persian boundary he entrusted to Bouzes, commanding him to take charge of the whole territory of the East until Belisarius should return from Italy. Bouzes therefore at first remained at Hierapolis, keeping his whole army with him; but when he learned what had befallen Sura, he called together the first men of the Hierapolitans and spoke as follows: "Whenever men are confronted with a struggle against an assailant with whom they are evenly matched in strength, it is not at all unreasonable that they should engage in open conflict with the enemy; but for those who are by comparison much inferior to their opponents it will be more advantageous to circumvent their enemy by some kind of tricks than to array themselves openly against them and thus enter into foreseen danger. How great, now, the army of Chosroes is you are assuredly informed. And if, with this army, he wishes to capture us by siege, and if we carry on the fight from the wall, it is probable that, while our supplies will fail us, the Persians will secure all they need from our land, where there will be no one to oppose them. And if the siege is prolonged in this way, I believe too that the fortification wall will not withstand the assaults of the enemy, for in many places it is most susceptible to attack, and thus irreparable harm will come to the Romans. But if with a portion of the army we guard the wall of the city, while the rest of us occupy the heights about the city, we shall make attacks from there at times upon the camp of our antagonists, and at times upon those who are sent out for the sake of provisions, and thus compel Chosroes to abandon the siege immediately and to make his retreat within a short time; for he will not be at all able to direct his attack without fear against the fortifications, nor to provide any of the necessities for so great an army." So spoke Bouzes; and in his words he seemed to set forth the advantageous course of action, but of what was necessary he did nothing. For he chose out all that portion of the Roman army which was of marked excellence and was off. And where in the world he was neither any of the Romans in Hierapolis, nor the hostile army was able to learn. Such, then, was the course of these events.

But the Emperor Justinian, upon learning of the inroad of the Persians, immediately sent his nephew Germanus with three hundred followers in great disorder, promising that after no great time a numerous army would follow. And Germanus, upon reaching Antioch, went around the whole circuit of the wall; and the greater part of it he found secure, for along that portion of it which lies on the level ground the River Orontes flows, making it everywhere difficult of access, and the portion which is on higher ground rises upon steep hills and is quite inaccessible to the enemy; but when he attained the highest point, which the men of that place are accustomed to call Orocasias, he noticed that the wall at that point was very easy to assail. For there happens to be in that place a rock, which spreads out to a very considerable width, and rises to a height only a little less than the fortifications. He therefore commanded that they should either cut off the rock by making a deep ditch along the wall, lest anyone should essay to mount from there upon the fortifications, or that they should build upon it a great tower and connect its structure with the wall of the city. But to the architects of public buildings it seemed that neither one of these things should be done. For, as they said, the work would not be completed in a short time with the attack of the enemy so imminent, while if they began this work and did not carry it to completion, they would do nothing else than shew to the enemy at what point in the wall they should make their attack. Germanus, though disappointed in this plan, had some hope at first because he expected an army from Byzantium. But when, after considerable time had passed, no army arrived from the emperor nor was expected to arrive, he began to fear lest Chosroes, learning that the emperor's nephew was there, would consider it more important than any other thing to capture Antioch and himself, and for this reason would neglect everything else and come against the city with his whole army. The natives of Antioch also had these things in mind, and they held a council concerning them, at which it seemed most advisable to offer money to Chosroes and thus escape the present danger.

Accordingly they sent Megas, the bishop of Beroea, a man of discretion who at that time happened to be tarrying among them, to beg for mercy from Chosroes; and departing from there he came upon the Median army not far from Hierapolis. And coming into the presence of Chosroes, he entreated him earnestly to have pity upon men who had committed no offence against him and who were not able to hold out against the Persian army. For it was becoming to a king least of all men to trample upon and do violence to those who retreated before him and were quite unwilling to array themselves against him; for not one of the things which he was then doing was a kingly or honourable act, because, without affording any time for consideration to the Roman emperor, so that he might either make the peace secure as might seem well to both sovereigns, or make his preparations for war in accordance with a mutual agreement, as was to be expected, he had thus recklessly advanced in arms against the Romans, while their emperor did not as yet know what had come upon them. When Chosroes heard this, he was utterly unable by reason of his stupidity to order his mind with reason and discretion, but still more than before he was lifted up in spirit. He therefore threatened to destroy all the Syrians and Cilicians, and bidding Megas follow him, he led his army to Hierapolis. When he had come there and established his camp, since he saw that the fortifications were strong and learned that the city was well garrisoned with soldiers, he demanded money from the Hierapolitans, sending to them Paulus as interpreter. This Paulus had been reared in Roman territory and had gone to an elementary school in Antioch, and besides he was said to be by birth of Roman extraction. But in spite of everything the inhabitants were exceedingly fearful for the fortifications, which embraced a large tract of land as far as the hill which rises there, and besides they wished to preserve their land unplundered; accordingly they agreed to give two thousand pounds of silver. Then indeed Megas entreated Chosroes in behalf of all the inhabitants of the East, and would not cease his entreaty, until Chosroes promised him that he would accept ten centenaria of gold and depart from the whole Roman empire.

VII

Thus, then, on that day Megas departed thence and went on the way to Antioch, while Chosroes after receiving the ransom was moving toward Beroea. This city lies between Antioch and Hierapolis, at a distance from both of two-days' journey for an unencumbered traveller. Now while Megas, who travelled with a small company, advanced very quickly, the Persian army was accomplishing only one half of the distance which he travelled each day. And so on the fourth day he reached Antioch, while the Persians came to the suburb of Beroea. And Chosroes immediately sent Paulus and demanded money of the Beroeans, not only as much as he had received from the Hierapolitans, but double the amount, since he saw that their wall in many places was very vulnerable. As for the Beroeans, since they could by no means place confidence in their fortifications, they gladly agreed to give all, but after giving two thousand pounds of silver, they said that they were not able to give the remainder. And since Chosroes pressed them on this account, on the following night all of them fled for refuge into the fortress which is on the acropolis together with the soldiers who had been stationed there to guard the place. And on the following day men were sent to the city by Chosroes in order to receive the money; but on coming near the fortifications they found all the gates closed, and being unable to discover any man, they reported the situation to the king. And he commanded them to set ladders against the wall and to make trial of mounting it, and they did as directed. Then since no one opposed them, they got inside the fortifications and opened the gates at their leisure, and received into the city the whole army and Chosroes himself. By this time the king was furious with anger and he fired nearly the whole city. He then mounted the acropolis and decided to storm the fortress. There indeed the Roman soldiers while valiantly defending themselves slew some of the enemy; but Chosroes was greatly favoured by fortune by reason of the folly of the besieged, who had not sought refuge in this fortress by themselves, but along with all their horses and other animals, and by this inconsiderate act they were placed at a great disadvantage and began to be in danger. For since there was only one spring there and the horses and mules and other animals drank from it when they should not have done so, it came about that the water was exhausted. Such, then, was the situation of the Beroeans.

Megas, upon reaching Antioch and announcing the terms arranged by him with Chosroes, failed utterly to persuade them to carry out this agreement. For it happened that the Emperor Justinian had sent John, the son of Rufinus, and Julian, his private[4] secretary, as ambassadors to Chosroes. The person holding this office is styled "a secretis" by the Romans; for secrets they are accustomed to call "secreta." These men had reached Antioch and were remaining there. Now Julian, one of the ambassadors, explicitly forbade everybody to give money to the enemy, or to purchase the cities of the emperor, and besides he denounced to Germanus the chief priest Ephraemius, as being eager to deliver over the city to Chosroes. For this reason Megas returned unsuccessful. But Ephraemius, the bishop of Antioch, fearing the attack of the Persians, went into Cilicia. There too came Germanus not long afterwards, taking with him some few men but leaving the most of them in Antioch.

Megas then came in haste to Beroea, and in vexation at what had taken place, he charged Chosroes with having treated the Beroeans outrageously; for while, as it seemed, he had sent him to Antioch to arrange the treaty, he had both plundered the property of the citizens, though they had committed no wrong at all, and had compelled them to shut themselves up in that fortress, and had then set fire to the city and razed it to the ground in defiance of right. To this Chosroes replied as follows: "Verily, my friend, you yourself are responsible for these things, in having compelled us to delay here; for as it is, you have arrived, not at the appointed time, but far behind it. And as for the strange conduct of your fellow-citizens, my most excellent sir, why should one make speeches of great length? For after agreeing to give us a fixed amount of silver for their own safety, they even now do not think it necessary to fulfil the agreement, but placing such complete confidence in the strength of their position, they are disregarding us absolutely, while we are compelled to undertake the siege of a fortress, as you surely see. But for my part, I have hope that with the help of the gods I shall have vengeance upon them shortly, and execute upon the guilty the punishment for the Persians whom I have lost wrongfully before this wall." So spoke Chosroes, and Megas replied as follows: "If one should consider that as king thou art making these charges against men who are in pitiable and most dishonoured plight, he would be compelled without a word of protest to agree with what thou hast said; for authority which is unlimited is bound by its very nature to carry with it also supremacy in argument; but if one be permitted to shake off all else and to espouse the truth of the matter, thou wouldst have, O King, nothing with which justly to reproach us; but mayst thou hear all mildly. First, as for me, since the time when I was sent to declare to the men of Antioch the message which thou didst send them, seven days have passed (and what could be done more quickly than this?) and now coming into thy presence I find these things accomplished by thee against my fatherland; but these men, having already lost all that is most valuable, thereafter have only one struggle to engage in, that for life, and have come, I think, so to be masters of the situation that they can no longer be compelled to pay thee any of the money. For to pay a thing which one does not possess could not be made possible for a man by any device. From of old indeed have the names of things been well and suitably distinguished by men; and among these distinctions is this, that want of power is separated from want of consideration. For when the latter by reason of intemperance of mind proceeds to resistance, it is accustomed to be detested, as is natural, but when the former, because of the impossibility of performing a service, is driven to the same point, it deserves to be pitied. Permit, therefore, O King, that, while we receive as our portion all the direst misfortunes, we may take with us this consolation at least, that we should not seem to have been ourselves responsible for the things which have befallen us. And as for money, consider that what thou hast taken into thy possession is sufficient for thee, not weighing this by thy position, but with regard to the power of the Beroeans. But beyond this do not force us in any way, lest perchance thou shouldst seem unable to accomplish the thing to which thou hast set thy hand; for excess is always punished by meeting obstacles that cannot be overcome, and the best course is not to essay the impossible. Let this, then, be my defence for the moment in behalf of these men. But if I should be able to have converse with the sufferers, I should have something else also to say which has now escaped me." So spoke Megas, and Chosroes permitted him to go into the acropolis. And when he had gone there and learned all that had happened concerning the spring, weeping he came again before Chosroes, and lying prone on the ground insisted that no money at all was left to the Beroeans, and entreated him to grant him only the lives of the men. Moved by the tearful entreaties of the man Chosroes fulfilled his request, and binding himself by an oath, gave pledges to all on the acropolis. Then the Beroeans, after coming into such great danger, left the acropolis free from harm, and departing went each his own way. Among the soldiers some few followed them, but the majority came as willing deserters to Chosroes, putting forth as their grievance that the government owed them their pay for a long time; and with him they later went into the land of Persia.

VIII

[June 540 A.D.] Then Chosroes (since Megas said that he had by no means persuaded the inhabitants of Antioch to bring him the money) went with his whole army against them. Some of the population of Antioch thereupon departed from there with their money and fled as each one could. And all the rest likewise were purposing to do the same thing, and would have done so had not the commanders of the troops in Lebanon, Theoctistus and Molatzes, who arrived in the meantime with six thousand men, fortified them with hope and thus prevented their departure. Not long after this the Persian army also came. There they all pitched their tents and made camp fronting on the River Orontes and not very far from the stream. Chosroes then sent Paulus up beside the fortifications and demanded money from the men of Antioch, saying that for ten centenaria[5] of gold he would depart from there, and it was obvious that he would accept even less than this for his withdrawal. And on that day their ambassadors went before Chosroes, and after speaking at length concerning the breaking of the peace and hearing much from him, they retired. But on the morrow the populace of Antioch (for they are not seriously disposed, but are always engaged in jesting and disorderly performance) heaped insults upon Chosroes from the battlements and taunted him with unseemly laughter; and when Paulus came near the fortifications and exhorted them to purchase freedom for themselves and the city for a small sum of money, they very nearly killed him with shots from their bows, and would have done so if he had not seen their purpose in time and guarded against it. On account of this Chosroes, boiling with anger, decided to storm the wall.

On the following day, accordingly, he led up all the Persians against the wall and commanded a portion of the army to make assaults at different points along the river, and he himself with the most of the men and best troops directed an attack against the height. For at this place, as has been stated by me above, the wall of fortification was most vulnerable. Thereupon the Romans, since the structure on which they were to stand when fighting was very narrow, devised the following remedy. Binding together long timbers they suspended them between the towers, and in this way they made these spaces much broader, in order that still more men might be able to ward off the assailants from there. So the Persians, pressing on most vigorously from all sides, were sending their arrows thickly everywhere, and especially along the crest of the hill. Meanwhile the Romans were fighting them back with all their strength, not soldiers alone, but also many of the most courageous youths of the populace. But it appeared that those who were attacking the wall there were engaged in a battle on even terms with their enemy. For the rock which was broad and high and, as it were, drawn up against the fortifications caused the conflict to be just as if on level ground. And if anyone of the Roman army had had the courage to get outside the fortifications with three hundred men and to anticipate the enemy in seizing this rock and to ward off the assailants from there, never, I believe, would the city have come into any danger from the enemy. For the barbarians had no point from which they could have conducted their assault, for they would be exposed to missiles from above both from the rock and from the wall; but as it was (for it was fated that Antioch be destroyed by this army of the Medes), this idea occurred to no one. So then while the Persians were fighting beyond their power, since Chosroes was present with them and urging them on with a mighty cry, giving their opponents not a moment in which to look about or guard against the missiles discharged from their bows, and while the Romans, in great numbers and with much shouting, were defending themselves still more vigorously, the ropes with which the beams had been bound together, failing to support the weight, suddenly broke asunder and the timbers together with all those who had taken their stand on them fell to the ground with a mighty crash. When this was heard by other Romans also, who were fighting from the adjoining towers, being utterly unable to comprehend what had happened, but supposing that the wall at this point had been destroyed, they beat a hasty retreat. Now many young men of the populace who in former times had been accustomed to engage in factional strife with each other in the hippodromes descended into the city from the fortification wall, but they refused to flee and remained where they were, while the soldiers with Theoctistus and Molatzes straightway leaped upon the horses which happened to be ready there and rode away to the gates, telling the others a tale to the effect that Bouzes had come with an army and they wished to receive them quickly into the city, and with them to ward off the enemy. Thereupon many of the men of Antioch and all the women with their children made a great rush toward the gates; but since they were crowded by the horses, being in very narrow quarters, they began to fall down. The soldiers, however, sparing absolutely no one of those before them, all kept riding over the fallen still more fiercely than before, and a great many were killed there, especially about the gates themselves.

But the Persians, with no one opposing them, set ladders against the wall and mounted with no difficulty. And quickly reaching the battlements, for a time they were by no means willing to descend, but they seemed like men looking about them and at a loss what to do, because, as it seems to me, they supposed that the rough ground was beset with some ambuscades of the enemy. For the land inside the fortifications which one traverses immediately upon descending from the height is an uninhabited tract extending for a great distance and there are found there rocks which rise to a very great height, and steep places. But some say that it was by the will of Chosroes that the Persians hesitated. For when he observed the difficulty of the ground and saw the soldiers fleeing, he feared lest by reason of some necessity they should turn back from their retreat and make trouble for the Persians, and thus become an obstacle, as might well happen, in the way of his capturing a city which was both ancient and of great importance and the first of all the cities which the Romans had throughout the East both in wealth and in size and in population and in beauty and in prosperity of every kind. Hence it was that, considering everything else of less account, he wished to allow the Roman soldiers freely to avail themselves of the chance for flight. For this reason too the Persians also made signs to the fugitives with their hands, urging them to flee as quickly as possible. So the soldiers of the Romans together with their commanders took a hasty departure, all of them, through the gate which leads to Daphne, the suburb of Antioch; for from this gate alone the Persians kept away while the others were seized; and of the populace some few escaped with the soldiers. Then when the Persians saw that all the Roman soldiers had gone on, they descended from the height and got into the middle of the city. There, however, many of the young men of Antioch engaged in battle with them, and at first they seemed to have the upper hand in the conflict. Some of them were in heavy armour, but the majority were unarmed and using only stones as missiles. And pushing back the enemy they raised the paean, and with shouts proclaimed the Emperor Justinian triumphant, as if they had won the victory.

At this point Chosroes, seated on the tower which is on the height, summoned the ambassadors, wishing to say something. And one of his officers, Zaberganes, thinking that he wished to have words with the ambassadors concerning a settlement, came quickly before the king and spoke as follows:

"Thou dost not seem to me, O Master, to think in the same way as do the Romans concerning the safety of these men. For they both before fighting offer insults to thy kingdom, and when they are defeated dare the impossible and do the Persians irreparable harm, as if fearing lest some reason for shewing them humanity should be left in thee; but thou art wishing to pity those who do not ask to be saved, and hast shewn zeal to spare those who by no means wish it. Meanwhile these men have set an ambush in a captured city and are destroying the victors by means of snares, although all the soldiers have long since fled from them." When Chosroes heard this, he sent a large number of the best troops against them, and these not long afterwards returned and announced that nothing untoward had come to pass. For already the Persians had forced back the citizens by their numbers and turned them to flight, and a great slaughter took place there. For the Persians did not spare persons of any age and were slaying all whom they met, old and young alike. At that time they say that two women of those who were illustrious in Antioch got outside the fortifications, but perceiving that they would fall into the hands of the enemy (for they were already plainly seen going about everywhere), went running to the River Orontes, and, fearing lest the Persians should do them some insult, they covered their faces with their veils and threw themselves into the river's current and were carried out of sight. Thus the inhabitants of Antioch were visited with every form of misfortune.

IX

Then Chosroes spoke to the ambassadors as follows: "Not far from the truth, I think, is the ancient saying that God does not give blessings unmixed, but He mingles them with troubles and then bestows them upon men. And for this reason we do not even have laughter without tears, but there is always attached to our successes some misfortune, and to our pleasures pain, not permitting anyone to enjoy in its purity such good fortune as is granted. For this city, which is of altogether preeminent importance in fact as well as in name in the land of the Romans I have indeed succeeded in capturing with the least exertion, since God has provided the victory all at once for us, as you doubtless see. But when I behold the massacre of such a multitude of men, and the victory thus drenched with blood, there arises in me no sense of the delight that should follow my achievement. And for this the wretched men of Antioch are to blame, for when the Persians were storming the wall they did not prove able to keep them back, and then when they had already triumphed and had captured the city at the first cry these men with unreasoned daring sought to die fighting against them in close combat. So while all the notables of the Persians were harassing me unceasingly with their demand that I should drag the city as with a net and destroy all the captives, I was commanding the fugitives to press on still more in their flight, in order that they might save themselves as quickly as possible. For to trample upon captives is not holy." Such high-sounding and airy words did Chosroes speak to the ambassadors, but nevertheless it did not escape them why he gave time to the Romans in their flight.

For he was the cleverest of all men at saying that which was not, and in concealing the truth, and in attributing the blame for the wrongs which he committed to those who suffered the wrong; besides he was ready to agree to everything and to pledge the agreement with an oath, and much more ready to forget completely the things lately agreed to and sworn to by him, and for the sake of money to debase his soul without reluctance to every act of pollution, a past master at feigning piety in his countenance, and absolving himself in words from the responsibility of the act. This man well displayed his own peculiar character on a certain occasion at Sura; for after he had hoodwinked the inhabitants of the city by a trick and had destroyed them in the manner which I have described, although they had previously done him no wrong at all, he saw, while the city was being captured, a comely woman and one not of lowly station being dragged by her left hand with great violence by one of the barbarians; and the child, which she had only lately weaned, she was unwilling to let go, but was dragging it with her other hand, fallen, as it was, to the ground since it was not able to keep pace with that violent running. And they say that he uttered a pretended groan, and making it appear to all who were present at that time including Anastasius the ambassador that he was all in tears, he prayed God to exact vengeance from the man who was guilty of the troubles which had come to pass. Now Justinian, the Emperor of the Romans, was the one whom he wished to have understood, though he knew well that he himself was most responsible for everything. Endowed with such a singular nature Chosroes both became King of the Persians (for ill fortune had deprived Zames of his eye, he who in point of years had first right to the kingdom, at any rate after Caoses, whom Cabades for no good reason hated), and with no difficulty he conquered those who revolted against him, and all the harm which he purposed to do the Romans he accomplished easily. For every time when Fortune wishes to make a man great, she does at the fitting times those things which she has decided upon, with no one standing against the force of her will; and she neither regards the man's station, nor purposes to prevent the occurrence of things which ought not to be, nor does she give heed that many will blaspheme against her because of these things, mocking scornfully at that which has been done by her contrary to the deserts of the man who receives her favour; nor does she take into consideration anything else at all, if only she accomplish the thing which has been decided upon by her. But as for these matters, let them be as God wishes.

Chosroes commanded the army to capture and enslave the survivors of the population of Antioch, and to plunder all the property, while he himself with the ambassadors descended from the height to the sanctuary which they call a church. There Chosroes found stores of gold and silver so great in amount that, though he took no other part of the booty except these stores, he departed possessed of enormous wealth. And he took down from there many wonderful marbles and ordered them to be deposited outside the fortifications, in order that they might convey these too to the land of Persia. When he had finished these things, he gave orders to the Persians to burn the whole city. And the ambassadors begged him to withhold his hand only from the church, for which he had carried away ransom in abundance. This he granted to the ambassadors, but gave orders to burn everything else; then, leaving there a few men who were to fire the city, he himself with all the rest retired to the camp where they had previously set up their tents.

X

A short time before this calamity God displayed a sign to the inhabitants of that city, by which He indicated the things which were to be. For the standards of the soldiers who had been stationed there for a long time had been standing previously toward the west, but of their own accord they turned and stood toward the east, and then returned again to their former position untouched by anyone. This the soldiers shewed to many who were near at hand and among them the manager of finances in the camp, while the standards were still trembling. This man, Tatianus by name, was an especially discreet person, a native of Mopsuestia. But even so those who saw this sign did not recognize that the mastery of the place would pass from the western to the eastern king, in order, evidently, that escape might be utterly impossible for those who were bound to suffer those things which came to pass.

But I become dizzy as I write of such a great calamity and transmit it to future times, and I am unable to understand why indeed it should be the will of God to exalt on high the fortunes of a man or of a place, and then to cast them down and destroy them for no cause which appears to us. For it is wrong to say that with Him all things are not always done with reason, though he then endured to see Antioch brought down to the ground at the hands of a most unholy man, a city whose beauty and grandeur in every respect could not even so be utterly concealed.

So, then, after the city had been destroyed, the church was left solitary, thanks to the activity and foresight of the Persians to whom this work was assigned. And there were also left about the so-called Cerataeum many houses, not because of the foresight of any man, but, since they were situated at the extremity of the city, and not connected with any other building, the fire failed entirely to reach them. The barbarians burned also the parts outside the fortifications, except the sanctuary which is dedicated to St. Julianus and the houses which stand about this sanctuary. For it happened that the ambassadors had taken up their lodgings there. As for the fortifications, the Persians left them wholly untouched.

A little later the ambassadors again came to Chosroes and spoke as follows: "If our words were not addressed to thee in thy presence, O King, we should never believe that Chosroes, the son of Cabades, had come into the land of the Romans in arms, dishonouring the oaths which have recently been sworn by thee, for such pledges are regarded as the last and most firm security of all things among men to guarantee mutual trust and truthfulness and breaking the treaty, though hope in treaties is the only thing left to those who are living in insecurity because of the evil deeds of war. For one might say of such a state of affairs that it is nothing else than the transformation of the habits of men into those of beasts. For in a time when no treaties at all are made, there will remain certainly war without end, and war which has no end is always calculated to estrange from their proper nature those who engage in it. With what intent, moreover, didst thou write to thy brother not long ago that he himself was responsible for the breaking of the treaty? Was it not obviously with the admission that the breaking of treaties is an exceedingly great evil? If therefore he has done no wrong, thou art not acting justly now in coming against us; but if it happen that thy brother has done any such thing, yet let thy complaint have its fulfilment thus far, and go no farther, that thou mayst shew thyself superior. For he who submits to be worsted in evil things would in better things justly be victorious. And yet we know well that the Emperor Justinian has never gone contrary to the treaty, and we entreat thee not to do the Romans such harm, from which there will be no advantage to the Persians, and thou wilt gain only this, that thou wilt have wrongfully wrought deeds of irreparable harm upon those who have recently made peace with thee." So spoke the ambassadors.

And Chosroes, upon hearing this, insisted that the treaty had been broken by the Emperor Justinian; and he enumerated the causes of war which the Emperor afforded, some of them of real importance and others idle and fabricated without any reason; most of all he wished to shew that the letters written by him to Alamoundaras and the Huns were the chief cause of the war, just as I have stated above[6]. But as for any Roman who had invaded the land of Persia, or who had made a display of warlike deeds, he was unable either to mention or to point out such a one. The ambassadors, however, referred the charges in part not to Justinian but to certain of those who had served him, while in the case of others they took exception to what he had said on the ground that the things had not taken place as stated. Finally Chosroes made the demand that the Romans give him a large sum of money, but he warned them not to hope to establish peace for all time by giving money at that moment only. For friendship, he said, which is made by men on terms of money is generally spent as fast as the money is used up. It was necessary, therefore, that the Romans should pay some definite annual sum to the Persians. "For thus," he said, "the Persians will keep the peace secure for them, guarding the Caspian Gates themselves and no longer feeling resentment at them on account of the city of Daras, in return for which the Persians themselves will be in their pay forever." "So," said the ambassadors, "the Persians desire to have the Romans subject and tributary to themselves." "No," said Chosroes, "but the Romans will have the Persians as their own soldiers for the future, dispensing to them a fixed payment for their service; for you give an annual payment of gold to some of the Huns and to the Saracens, not as tributary subjects to them, but in order that they may guard your land unplundered for all time." After Chosroes and the ambassadors had spoken thus at length with each other, they at last came to terms, agreeing that Chosroes should forthwith take from the Romans fifty centenaria[7], and that, receiving a tribute of five more centenaria annually for all time, he should do them no further harm, but taking with him hostages from the ambassadors to pledge the keeping of the agreement, should make his departure with the whole army to his native land, and that there ambassadors sent from the Emperor Justinian should arrange on a firm basis for the future the compact regarding the peace.

XI

Then Chosroes went to Seleucia, a city on the sea, one hundred and thirty stades distant from Antioch; and there he neither met nor harmed a single Roman, and he bathed himself alone in the sea-water, and after sacrificing to the sun and such other divinities as he wished, and calling upon the gods many times, he went back. And when he came to the camp, he said that he had a desire to see the city of Apamea which was in the vicinity for no other reason than that of his interest in the place. And the ambassadors unwillingly granted this also, but only on condition that after seeing the city and taking away with him from there one thousand pounds of silver, he should, without inflicting any further injury, march back. But it was evident to the ambassadors and to all the others that Chosroes was setting out for Apamea with this sole purpose, that he might lay hold upon some pretext of no importance and plunder both the city and the land thereabout. Accordingly he first went up to Daphne, the suburb of Antioch, where he expressed great wonder at the grove and at the fountains of water; for both of these are very well worth seeing. And after sacrificing to the nymphs he departed, doing no further damage than burning the sanctuary of the archangel Michael together with certain other buildings, for the following reason. A Persian gentleman of high repute in the army of the Persians and well known to Chosroes, the king, while riding on horseback came in company with some others to a precipitous place near the so-called Tretum, where is a temple of the archangel Michael, the work of Evaris. This man, seeing one of the young men of Antioch on foot and alone concealing himself there, separated from the others and pursued him. Now the young man was a butcher, Aeimachus by name. When he was about to be overtaken, he turned about unexpectedly and threw a stone at his pursuer which hit him on the forehead and penetrated to the membrane by the ear. And the rider fell immediately to the ground, whereupon the youth drew out his sword and slew him. Then at his leisure he stripped him of his weapons and all his gold and whatever else he had on his person, and leaping upon his horse rode on. And whether by the favour of fortune or by his knowledge of the country, he succeeded completely in eluding the Persians and making good his escape. When Chosroes learned this, he was deeply grieved at what had happened, and commanded some of his followers to burn the sanctuary of the archangel Michael which I have mentioned above. And they, thinking that the sanctuary at Daphne was the one in question, burned it with the buildings about it, and they supposed that the commands of Chosroes had been executed. Such, then, was the course of these events.

But Chosroes with his whole army proceeded on the way to Apamea. Now there is a piece of wood one cubit in length in Apamea, a portion of the cross on which the Christ in Jerusalem once endured the punishment not unwillingly, as is generally agreed, and which in ancient times had been conveyed there secretly by a man of Syria. And the men of olden times, believing that it would be a great protection both for themselves and for the city, made for it a sort of wooden chest and deposited it there; and they adorned this chest with much gold and with precious stones and they entrusted it to three priests who were to guard it in all security; and they bring it forth every year and the whole population worship it during one day. Now at that time the people of Apamea, upon learning that the army of the Medes was coming against them, began to be in great fear. And when they heard that Chosroes was absolutely untruthful, they came to Thomas, the chief priest of the city, and begged him to shew them the wood of the cross, in order that after worshipping it for the last time they might die. And he did as they requested. Then indeed it befell that a sight surpassing both description and belief was there seen. For while the priest was carrying the wood and shewing it, above him followed a flame of fire, and the portion of the roof over him was illuminated with a great and unaccustomed light. And while the priest was moving through every part of the temple, the flame continued to advance with him, keeping constantly the place above him in the roof. So the people of Apamea, under the spell of joy at the miracle, were wondering and rejoicing and weeping, and already all felt confidence concerning their safety. And Thomas, after going about the whole temple, laid the wood of the cross in the chest and covered it, and suddenly the light had ceased. Then upon learning that the army of the enemy had come close to the city, he went in great haste to Chosroes. And when the king enquired of the priest whether it was the will of the citizens of Apamea to marshal themselves on the wall against the army of the Medes, the priest replied that no such thing had entered the minds of the men. "Therefore," said Chosroes, "receive me into the city accompanied by a few men with all the gates opened wide." And the priest said "Yes, for I have come here to invite thee to do this very thing." So the whole army pitched their tents and made camp before the fortifications.

Then Chosroes chose out two hundred of the best of the Persians and entered the city. But when he had got inside the gates, he forgot willingly enough what had been agreed upon between himself and the ambassadors, and he commanded the bishop to give not only one thousand pounds of silver nor even ten times that amount, but whatsoever treasures were stored there, being all of gold and silver and of marvellous great size. And I believe that he would not have shrunk from enslaving and plundering the whole city, unless some divine providence had manifestly prevented him; to such a degree did avarice overpower him and the desire of fame turn his mind. For he thought the enslavement of the cities a great glory for himself, considering it absolutely nothing that disregarding treaties and compacts he was performing such deeds against the Romans. This attitude of Chosroes will be revealed by what he undertook to do concerning the city of Daras during his withdrawal at this same time, when he treated his agreements with absolute disregard, and also by what he did to the citizens of Callinicus a little later in time of peace, as will be told by me in the following narrative[8]. But God, as has been said, preserved Apamea. Now when Chosroes had seized all the treasures, and Thomas saw that he was already intoxicated with the abundance of the wealth, then bringing out the wood of the cross with the chest, he opened the chest and displaying the wood said: "O most mighty King, these alone are left me out of all the treasures. Now as for this chest (since it is adorned with gold and precious stones), we do not begrudge thy taking it and keeping it with all the rest, but this wood here, it is our salvation and precious to us, this, I beg and entreat thee, give to me." So spoke the priest. And Chosroes yielded and fulfilled the request.

Afterwards, being filled with a desire for popular applause, he commanded that the populace should go up into the hippodrome and that the charioteers should hold their accustomed contests. And he himself went up there also, eager to be a spectator of the performances. And since he had heard long before that the Emperor Justinian was extraordinarily fond of the Venetus[9] colour, which is blue, wishing to go against him there also, he was desirous of bringing about victory for the green. So the charioteers, starting from the barriers, began the contest, and by some chance he who was clad in the blue happened to pass his rival and take the lead. And he was followed in the same tracks by the wearer of the green colour. And Chosroes, thinking that this had been done purposely, was angry, and he cried out with a threat that the Caesar had wrongfully surpassed the others, and he commanded that the horses which were running in front should be held up, in order that from then on they might contend in the rear; and when this had been done just as he commanded, then Chosroes and the green faction were accounted victorious. At that time one of the citizens of Apamea came before Chosroes and accused a Persian of entering his house and violating his maiden daughter. Upon hearing this, Chosroes, boiling with anger, commanded that the man should be brought. And when he came before him, he directed that he should be impaled in the camp. And when the people learned this, they raised a mighty shout as loud as they could, demanding that the man be saved from the king's anger. And Chosroes promised that he would release the man to them, but he secretly impaled him not long afterwards. So after these things had been thus accomplished, he departed and marched back with the whole army.

XII

And when he came to the city of Chalcis, eighty-four stades distant from the city of Beroea, he again seemed to forget the things which had been agreed upon, and encamping not far from the fortifications he sent Paulus to threaten the inhabitants of Chalcis, saying that he would take the city by siege, unless they should purchase their safety by giving ransom, and should give up to the Persians all the soldiers who were there together with their leader. And the citizens of Chalcis were seized with great fear of both sovereigns, and they swore that, as for soldiers, there were absolutely none of them in the city, although they had hidden Adonachus, the commander of the soldiers, and others as well in some houses, in order that they might not be seen by the enemy; and with difficulty they collected two centenaria[10] of gold, for the city they inhabited was not very prosperous, and they gave them to Chosroes as the price of their lives and thus saved both the city and themselves.

From there on Chosroes did not wish to continue the return journey by the road he had come, but to cross the River Euphrates and gather by plunder as much money as possible from Mesopotamia. He therefore constructed a bridge at the place called Obbane, which is forty stades distant from the fortress in Barbalissum; then he himself went across and gave orders to the whole army to cross as quickly as possible, adding that he would break up the bridge on the third day, and he appointed also the time of the day. And when the appointed day was come, it happened that some of the army were left who had not yet crossed, but without the least consideration for them he sent the men to break up the bridge. And those who were left behind returned to their native land as each one could.

Then a sort of ambition came over Chosroes to capture the city of Edessa. For he was led on to this by a saying of the Christians, and it kept irritating his mind, because they maintained that it could not be taken, for the following reason. There was a certain Augarus in early times, toparch of Edessa (for thus the kings of the different nations were called then). Now this Augarus was the most clever of all men of his time, and as a result of this was an especial friend of the Emperor Augustus. For, desiring to make a treaty with the Romans, he came to Rome; and when he conversed with Augustus, he so astonished him by the abundance of his wisdom that Augustus wished never more to give up his company; for he was an ardent lover of his conversation, and whenever he met him, he was quite unwilling to depart from him. A long time, therefore, was consumed by him in this visit. And one day when he was desirous of returning to his native land and was utterly unable to persuade Augustus to let him go, he devised the following plan. He first went out to hunt in the country about Rome; for it happened that he had taken considerable interest in the practice of this sport. And going about over a large tract of country, he captured alive many of the animals of that region, and he gathered up and took with him from each part of the country some earth from the land; thus he returned to Rome bringing both the earth and the animals. Then Augustus went up into the hippodrome and seated himself as was his wont, and Augarus came before him and displayed the earth and the animals, telling over from what district each portion of earth was and what animals they were. Then he gave orders to put the earth in different parts of the hippodrome, and to gather all the animals into one place and then to release them. So the attendants did as he directed. And the animals, separating from each other, went each to that portion of earth which was from the district in which it itself had been taken. And Augustus looked upon the performance carefully for a very long time, and he was wondering that nature untaught makes animals miss their native land. Then Augarus, suddenly laying hold upon his knees, said: "But as for me, O Master, what thoughts dost thou think I have, who possess a wife and children and a kingdom, small indeed, but in the land of my fathers?" And the emperor, overcome and compelled by the truth of his saying, granted not at all willingly that he should go away, and bade him ask besides whatever he wished. And when Augarus had secured this, he begged of Augustus to build him a hippodrome in the city of Edessa. And he granted also this. Thus then Augarus departed from Rome and came to Edessa. And the citizens enquired of him whether he had come bringing any good thing for them from the Emperor Augustus. And he answering said he had brought to the inhabitants of Edessa pain without loss and pleasure without gain, hinting at the fortune of the hippodrome.

At a later time when Augarus was well advanced in years, he was seized with an exceedingly violent attack of gout. And being distressed by the pains and his inability to move in consequence of them, he carried the matter to the physicians, and from the whole land he gathered all who were skilled in these matters. But later he abandoned these men (for they did not succeed in discovering any cure for the trouble), and finding himself helpless, he bewailed the fate which was upon him. But about that time Jesus, the Son of God, was in the body and moving among the men of Palestine, shewing manifestly by the fact that he never sinned at all, and also by his performing even things impossible, that he was the Son of God in very truth; for he called the dead and raised them up as if from sleep, and opened the eyes of men who had been born blind, and cleansed those whose whole bodies were covered with leprosy, and released those whose feet were maimed, and he cured all the other diseases which are called by the physicians incurable. When these things were reported to Augarus by those who travelled from Palestine to Edessa, he took courage and wrote a letter to Jesus, begging him to depart from Judaea and the senseless people there, and to spend his life with him from that time forward. When the Christ saw this message, he wrote in reply to Augarus, saying distinctly that he would not come, but promising him health in the letter. And they say that he added this also that never would the city be liable to capture by the barbarians. This final portion of the letter was entirely unknown to those who wrote the history of that time; for they did not even make mention of it anywhere; but the men of Edessa say that they found it with the letter, so that they have even caused the letter to be inscribed in this form on the gates of the city instead of any other defence. The city did in fact come under the Medes a short time afterwards, not by capture however, but in the following manner. A short time after Augarus received the letter of the Christ, he became free from suffering, and after living on in health for a long time, he came to his end. But that one of his sons who succeeded to the kingdom shewed himself the most unholy of all men, and besides committing many other wrongs against his subjects, he voluntarily went over to the Persians, fearing the vengeance which was to come from the Romans. But long after this the citizens of Edessa destroyed the barbarian guards who were dwelling with them, and gave the city into the hands of the Romans. * * *[11] he is eager to attach it to his cause, judging by what has happened in my time, which I shall present in the appropriate place. And the thought once occurred to me that, if the Christ did not write this thing just as I have told it, still, since men have come to believe in it, He wishes to guard the city uncaptured for this reason, that He may never give them any pretext for error. As for these things, then, let them be as God wills, and so let them be told.

For this reason it seemed to Chosroes at that time a matter of moment to capture Edessa. And when he came to Batne, a small stronghold of no importance, one day's journey distant from Edessa, he bivouacked there for that night, but at early dawn he was on the march to Edessa with his whole army. But it fell out that they lost their way and wandered about, and on the following night bivouacked in the same place; and they say that this happened to them a second time also. When with difficulty Chosroes reached the neighbourhood of Edessa, they say that suppuration set in in his face and his jaw became swollen. For this reason he was quite unwilling to make an attempt on the city, but he sent Paulus and demanded money from the citizens. And they said that they had absolutely no fear concerning the city, but in order that he might not damage the country they agreed to give two centenaria of gold. And Chosroes took the money and kept the agreement.

XIII

At that time also the Emperor Justinian wrote a letter to Chosroes, promising to carry out the agreement which had been made by him and the ambassadors regarding the peace[12]. When this message was received by Chosroes, he released the hostages and made preparations for his departure, and he wished to sell off all the captives from Antioch. And when the citizens of Edessa learned of this, they displayed an unheard-of zeal. For there was not a person who did not bring ransom for the captives and deposit it in the sanctuary according to the measure of his possessions. And there were some who even exceeded their proportionate amount in so doing. For the harlots took off all the adornment which they wore on their persons, and threw it down there, and any farmer who was in want of plate or of money, but who had an ass or a sheep, brought this to the sanctuary with great zeal. So there was collected an exceedingly great amount of gold and silver and money in other forms, but not a bit of it was given for ransom. For Bouzes happened to be present there, and he took in hand to prevent the transaction, expecting that this would bring him some great gain. Therefore Chosroes moved forward, taking with him all the captives. And the citizens of Carrhae met him holding out to him great sums of money; but he said that it did not belong to him because the most of them are not Christians but are of the old faith.

But when, likewise, the citizens of Constantina offered money, he accepted it, although he asserted that the city belonged to him from his fathers. [503 A.D.] For at the time when Cabades took Amida, he wished also to capture Edessa and Constantina. But when he came near to Edessa he enquired of the Magi whether it would be possible for him to capture the city, pointing out the place to them with his right hand. But they said that the city would not be captured by him by any device, judging by the fact that in stretching out his right hand to it he was not giving thereby the sign of capture or of any other grievous thing, but of salvation. And when Cabades heard this, he was convinced and led his army on to Constantina. And upon arriving there, he issued orders to the whole army to encamp for a siege. Now the priest of Constantina was at that time Baradotus, a just man and especially beloved of God, and his prayers for this reason were always effectual for whatever he wished; and even seeing his face one would have straightway surmised that this man was most completely acceptable to God. This Baradotus came then to Cabades bearing wine and dried figs and honey and unblemished loaves, and entreated him not to make an attempt on a city which was not of any importance and which was very much neglected by the Romans, having neither a garrison of soldiers nor any other defence, but only the inhabitants, who were pitiable folk. Thus spoke the priest; and Cabades promised that he would grant him the city freely, and he presented him with all the food-supplies which had been prepared by him for the army in anticipation of the siege, an exceedingly great quantity; and thus he departed from the land of the Romans. For this reason it was that Chosroes claimed that the city belonged to him from his fathers.

And when he reached Daras, he began a siege; but within the city the Romans and Martinus, their general (for it happened that he was there), made their preparations for resistance. Now the city is surrounded by two walls, the inner one of which is of great size and a truly wonderful thing to look upon (for each tower reaches to a height of a hundred feet, and the rest of the wall to sixty), while the outer wall is much smaller, but in other respects strong and one to be reckoned with seriously. And the space between has a breadth of not less than fifty feet; in that place the citizens of Daras are accustomed to put their cattle and other animals when an enemy assails them. At first then Chosroes made an assault on the fortifications toward the west, and forcing back his opponents by overwhelming numbers of missiles, he set fire to the gates of the small wall. However no one of the barbarians dared to get inside. Next he decided to make a tunnel secretly at the eastern side of the city. For at this point alone can the earth be dug, since the other parts of the fortifications were set upon rock by the builders. So the Persians began to dig, beginning from their trench. And since this was very deep, they were neither observed by the enemy nor did they afford them any means of discovering what was being done. So they had already gone under the foundations of the outer wall, and were about to reach the space between the two walls and soon after to pass also the great wall and take the city by force; but since it was not fated to be captured by the Persians, someone from the camp of Chosroes came alone about midday close to the fortifications, whether a man or something else greater than man, and he made it appear to those who saw him that he was collecting the weapons which the Romans had a little before discharged from the wall against the barbarians who were assailing them. And while doing this and holding his shield before him, he seemed to be bantering those who were on the parapet and taunting them with laughter. Then he told them of everything and commanded them all to be on the watch and to take all possible care for their safety. After revealing these things he was off, while the Romans with much shouting and confusion were ordering men to dig the ground between the two walls. The Persians, on the other hand, not knowing what was being done, were pushing on the work no less than before. So while the Persians were making a straight way underground to the wall of the city, the Romans by the advice of Theodoras, a man learned in the science called mechanics, were constructing their trench in a cross-wise direction and making it of sufficient depth, so that when the Persians had reached the middle point between the two circuit-walls they suddenly broke into the trench of the Romans. And the first of them the Romans killed, while those in the rear by fleeing at top speed into the camp saved themselves. For the Romans decided by no means to pursue them in the dark. So Chosroes, failing in this attempt and having no hope that he would take the city by any device thereafter, opened negotiations with the besieged, and carrying away a thousand pounds of silver he retired into the land of Persia. When this came to the knowledge of the Emperor Justinian, he was no longer willing to carry the agreement into effect, charging Chosroes with having attempted to capture the city of Daras during a truce. Such were the fortunes of the Romans during the first invasion of Chosroes; and the summer drew to its close.

XIV

Now Chosroes built a city in Assyria in a place one day's journey distant from the city of Ctesiphon, and he named it the Antioch of Chosroes and settled there all the captives from Antioch, constructing for them a bath and a hippodrome and providing that they should have free enjoyment of their other luxuries besides. For he brought with him charioteers and musicians both from Antioch and from the other Roman cities. Besides this he always provisioned these citizens of Antioch at public expense more carefully than in the fashion of captives, and he required that they be called king's subjects, so as to be subordinate to no one of the magistrates, but to the king alone. And if anyone else too who was a Roman in slavery ran away and succeeded in escaping to the Antioch of Chosroes, and if he was called a kinsman by any one of those who lived there, it was no longer possible for the owner of this captive to take him away, not even if he who had enslaved the man happened to be a person of especial note among the Persians.

Thus, then, the portent which had come to the citizens of Antioch in the reign of Anastasius reached this final fulfilment for them. For at that time a violent wind suddenly fell upon the suburb of Daphne, and some of the cypresses which were there of extraordinary height were overturned from the extremities of their roots and fell to the earth, trees which the law forbade absolutely to be cut down. [526 A.D.] Accordingly, a little later, when Justinus was ruling over the Romans, the place was visited by an exceedingly violent earthquake, which shook down the whole city and straightway brought to the ground the most and the finest of the buildings, and it is said that at that time three hundred thousand of the population of Antioch perished. And finally in this capture the whole city, as has been said, was destroyed. Such, then, was the calamity which befell the men of Antioch.

And Belisarius came to Byzantium from Italy, summoned by the emperor; and after he had spent the winter in Byzantium, the emperor sent him as general against Chosroes and the Persians at the opening of spring, together with the officers who had come with him from Italy, one of whom, Valerianus, he commanded to lead the troops in Armenia. [541 A.D.] For Martinus had been sent immediately to the East, and for this reason Chosroes found him at Daras, as has been stated above. And among the Goths, Vittigis remained in Byzantium, but all the rest marched with Belisarius against Chosroes. At that time one of the envoys of Vittigis, he who was assuming the name of bishop, died in the land of Persia, and the other one remained there. And the man who followed them as interpreter withdrew to the land of the Romans, and John, who was commanding the troops in Mesopotamia, arrested him near the boundaries of Constantina, and bringing him into the city confined him in a prison; there the man in answer to his enquiries related everything which had been done. Such, then, was the course of these events. And Belisarius and his followers went in haste, since he was eager to anticipate Chosroes' making any second invasion into the land of the Romans.

XV

But in the meantime Chosroes was leading his army against Colchis, where the Lazi were calling him in for the following reason. The Lazi at first dwelt in the land of Colchis as subjects of the Romans, but not to the extent of paying them tribute or obeying their commands in any respect, except that, whenever their king died, the Roman emperor would send emblems of the office to him who was about to succeed to the throne. And he, together with his subjects, guarded strictly the boundaries of the land in order that hostile Huns might not proceed from the Caucasus mountains, which adjoin their territory, through Lazica and invade the land of the Romans. And they kept guard without receiving money or troops from the Romans and without ever joining the Roman armies, but they were always engaged in commerce by sea with the Romans who live on the Black Sea. For they themselves have neither salt nor grain nor any other good thing, but by furnishing skins and hides and slaves they secured the supplies which they needed. But when the events came to pass in which Gourgenes, the king of the Iberians, was concerned, as has been told in the preceding narrative[13], Roman soldiers began to be quartered among the Lazi; and these barbarians were annoyed by the soldiers, and most of all by Peter, the general, a man who was prone to treat insolently those who came into contact with him. This Peter was a native of Arzanene, which is beyond the River Nymphius, a district subject to the Persians from of old, but while still a child he had been captured and enslaved by the Emperor Justinus at the time when Justinus, after the taking of Amida, was invading the land of the Persians with Celer's army.[14] And since his owner showed him great kindness, he attended the school of a grammatist. And at first he became secretary to Justinus, but when, after the death of Anastasius, Justinus took over the Roman empire, Peter was made a general, and he degenerated into a slave of avarice, if anyone ever did, and shewed himself very fatuous in his treatment of all.

And later the Emperor Justinian sent different officers to Lazica, and among them John, whom they called Tzibus, a man of obscure and ignoble descent, but who had climbed to the office of general by virtue of no other thing than that he was the most accomplished villain in the world and most successful in discovering unlawful sources of revenue. This man unsettled and threw into confusion all the relations of the Romans and the Lazi. He also persuaded the Emperor Justinian to build a city on the sea in Lazica, Petra by name; and there he sat as in a citadel and plundered the property of the Lazi. For the salt, and all other cargoes which were considered necessary for the Lazi, it was no longer possible for the merchants to bring into the land of Colchis, nor could they purchase them elsewhere by sending for them, but he set up in Petra the so-called "monopoly" and himself became a retail dealer and overseer of all the handling of these things, buying everything and selling it to the

Colchians, not at the customary rates, but as dearly as possible. At the same time, even apart from this, the barbarians were annoyed by the Roman army quartered upon them, a thing which had not been customary previously. Accordingly, since they were no longer able to endure these things, they decided to attach themselves to the Persians and Chosroes, and immediately they sent to them envoys who were to arrange this without the knowledge of the Romans. These men had been instructed that they should take pledges from Chosroes that he would never give up the Lazi against their will to the Romans, and that with this understanding they should bring him with the Persian army into the land.

Accordingly the envoys went to the Persians, and coming secretly before Chosroes they said: "If any people in all time have revolted from their own friends in any manner whatsoever and attached themselves wrongfully to men utterly unknown to them, and after that by the kindness of fortune have been brought back once more with greatest rejoicing to those who were formerly their own, consider, O Most mighty King, that such as these are the Lazi. For the Colchians in ancient times, as allies of the Persians, rendered them many good services and were themselves treated in like manner; and of these things there are many records in books, some of which we have, while others are preserved in thy palace up to the present time. But at a later time it came about that our ancestors, whether neglected by you or for some other reason (for we are unable to ascertain anything certain about this matter), became allies of the Romans. And now we and the king of Lazica give to the Persians both ourselves and our land to treat in any way you may desire. And we beg of you to think thus concerning us: if, on the one hand, we have suffered nothing outrageous at the hands of the Romans, but have been prompted by foolish motives in coming to you, reject this prayer of ours straightway, considering that with you likewise the Colchians will never be trustworthy (for when a friendship has been dissolved, a second friendship formed with others becomes, owing to its character, a matter of reproach); but if we have been in name friends of the Romans, but in fact their loyal slaves, and have suffered impious treatment at the hands of those who have tyrannized over us, receive us, your former allies, and acquire as slaves those whom you used to treat as friends, and shew your hatred of a cruel tyranny which has risen thus on our borders, by acting worthily of that justice which it has always been the tradition of the Persians to defend. For the man who himself does no wrong is not just, unless he is also accustomed to rescue those who are wronged by others when he has it in his power. But it is worth while to tell a few of the things which the accursed Romans have dared to do against us. In the first place they have left our king only the form of royal power, while they themselves have appropriated the actual authority, and he sits a king in the position of a servant, fearing the general who issues the orders; and they have put upon us a multitude of soldiery, not in order to guard the land against those who harass us (for not one of our neighbours except, indeed, the Romans has disturbed us), but in order that they may confine us as in a prison and make themselves masters of our possessions. And purposing to make more speedy the robbery of what we have, behold, O King, what sort of a design they have formed; the supplies which are in excess among them they compel the Lazi to buy against their will, while those things which are most useful to them among the products of Lazica these fellows demand to buy, as they put it, from us, the price being determined in both cases by the judgment of the stronger party. And thus they are robbing us of all our gold as well as of the necessities of life, using the fair name of trade, but in fact oppressing us as thoroughly as they possibly can. And there has been set over us as ruler a huckster who has made our destitution a kind of business by virtue of the authority of his office. The cause of our revolt, therefore, being of this sort, has justice on its side; but the advantage which you yourselves will gain if you receive the request of the Lazi we shall forthwith tell. To the realm of Persia you will add a most ancient kingdom, and as a result of this you will have the power of your sway extended, and it will come about that you will have a part in the sea of the Romans through our land, and after thou hast built ships in this sea, O King, it will be possible for thee with no trouble to set foot in the palace in Byzantium. For there is no obstacle between. And one might add that the plundering of the land of the Romans every year by the barbarians along the boundary will be under your control. For surely you also are acquainted with the fact that up till now the land of the Lazi has been a bulwark against the Caucasus mountains. So with justice leading the way, and advantage added thereto, we consider that not to receive our words with favour would be wholly contrary to good judgment." So spoke the envoys.

And Chosroes, delighted by their words, promised to protect the Lazi, and enquired of the envoys whether it was possible for him to enter the land of Colchis with a large army. For he said that previously he had heard many persons report that the land was exceedingly hard to traverse even for an unimpeded traveller, being extremely rugged and covered very extensively by thick forests of wide-spreading trees. But the envoys stoutly maintained to him that the way through the country would be easy for the whole Persian army, if they cut the trees and threw them into the places which were made difficult by precipices. And they promised that they themselves would be guides of the route, and would take the lead in this work for the Persians. Encouraged by this suggestion, Chosroes gathered a great army and made his preparations for the inroad, not disclosing the plan to the Persians except those alone to whom he was accustomed to communicate his secrets, and commanding the envoys to tell no one what was being done; and he pretended that he was setting out into Iberia, in order to settle matters there; for a Hunnic tribe, he kept saying in explanation, had assailed the Persian domain at that point.

XVI

At this time Belisarius had arrived in Mesopotamia and was gathering his army from every quarter, and he also kept sending men into the land of Persia to act as spies. And wishing himself to encounter the enemy there, if they should again make an incursion into the land of the Romans, he was organizing on the spot and equipping the soldiers, who were for the most part without either arms or armour, and in terror of the name of the Persians. Now the spies returned and declared that for the present there would be no invasion of the enemy; for Chosroes was occupied elsewhere with a war against the Huns. And Belisarius, upon learning this, wished to invade the land of the enemy immediately with his whole army. Arethas also came to him with a large force of Saracens, and besides the emperor wrote a letter instructing him to invade the enemy's country with all speed. He therefore called together all the officers in Daras and spoke as follows: "I know that all of you, my fellow officers, are experienced in many wars, and I have brought you together at the present time, not in order to stir up your minds against the enemy by addressing to you any reminder or exhortation (for I think that you need no speech that prompts to daring), but in order that we may deliberate together among ourselves, and choose rather the course which may seem fairest and best for the cause of the emperor. For war is wont to succeed by reason of careful planning more than by anything else. Now it is necessary that those who gather for deliberation should make their minds entirely free from modesty and from fear. For fear, by paralyzing those who have fallen into it, does not allow the reason to choose the nobler part, and modesty obscures what has been seen to be the better course and leads investigation the opposite way. If, therefore, it seems to you that any purpose has been formed either by our mighty emperor or by me concerning the present situation, let no thought of this enter your minds. For, as for him, he is altogether ignorant of what is being done, and is therefore unable to adapt his moves to opportune moments; there is therefore no fear but that in going contrary to him we shall do that which will be of advantage to his cause. And as for me, since I am human, and have come here from the West after a long interval, it is impossible that some of the necessary things should not escape me. So it behoves you, without any too modest regard for my opinion, to say outright whatever is going to be of advantage for ourselves and for the emperor. Now in the beginning, fellow officers, we came here in order to prevent the enemy from making any invasion into our land, but at the present time, since things have gone better for us than we had hoped, it is possible for us to make his land the subject of our deliberation. And now that you have been gathered together for this purpose, it is fair, I think, that you should tell without any concealment what seems to each one best and most advantageous." Thus spoke Belisarius.

And Peter and Bouzes urged him to lead the army without any hesitation against the enemy's country. And their opinion was followed immediately by the whole council. Rhecithancus, however, and Theoctistus, the commanders of the troops in Lebanon, said that, while they too had the same wish as the others concerning the invasion, they feared that if they abandoned the country of Phoenicia and Syria, Alamoundaras would plunder it at his leisure, and that the emperor would be angry with them because they had not guarded and kept unplundered the territory under their command, and for this reason they were quite unwilling to join the rest of the army in the invasion. But Belisarius said that the opinion of these two men was not in the least degree true; for it was the season of the vernal equinox, and at this season the Saracens always dedicated about two months to their god, and during this time never undertook any inroad into the land of others. Agreeing, therefore, to release both of them with their followers within sixty days, he commanded them also to follow with the rest of the army. So Belisarius was making his preparation for the invasion with great zeal.

XVII

But Chosroes and the Median army, after crossing Iberia, reached the territory of Lazica under the leadership of the envoys; there with no one to withstand them they began to cut down the trees which grow thickly over that very mountainous region, rising to a great height, and spreading out their branches remarkably, so that they made the country absolutely impassable for the army; and these they threw into the rough places, and thus rendered the road altogether easy. And when they arrived in the centre of Colchis (the place where the tales of the poets say that the adventure of Medea and Jason took place), Goubazes, the king of the Lazi, came and did obeisance to Chosroes, the son of Cabades, as Lord, putting himself together with his palace and all Lazica into his hand.

Now there is a coast city named Petra in Colchis, on the sea which is called the Euxine, which in former times had been a place of no importance, but which the Emperor Justinian had rendered strong and otherwise conspicuous by means of the circuit-wall and other buildings which he erected. When Chosroes ascertained that the Roman army was in that place with John, he sent an army and a general, Aniabedes, against them in order to capture the place at the first onset. But John, upon learning of their approach, gave orders that no one should go outside the fortifications nor allow himself to be seen from the parapet by the enemy, and he armed the whole army and stationed them in the vicinity of the gates, commanding them to keep silence and not allow the least sound of any kind to escape from them. So the Persians came close to the fortifications, and since nothing of the enemy was either seen or heard by them they thought that the Romans had abandoned the city and left it destitute of men. For this reason they closed in still more around the fortifications, so as to set up ladders immediately, since no one was defending the wall. And neither seeing nor hearing anything of the enemy, they sent to Chosroes and explained the situation. And he sent the greater part of the army, commanding them to make an attempt upon the fortifications from all sides, and he directed one of the officers to make use of the engine known as a ram around the gate, while he himself, seated on the hill which lies very close to the city, became a spectator of the operations. And straightway the Romans opened the gates all of a sudden, and unexpectedly fell upon and slew great numbers of the enemy, and especially those stationed about the ram; the rest with difficulty made their escape together with the general and were saved. And Chosroes, filled with rage, impaled Aniabedes, since he had been outgeneralled by John, a tradesman and an altogether unwarlike man. But some say that not Aniabedes, but the officer commanding the men who were working the ram was impaled. And he himself broke camp with the whole army, and coming close to the fortifications of Petra, made camp and began a siege. On the following day he went completely around the fortifications, and since he suspected that they could not support a very strong attack, he decided to storm the wall. And bringing up the whole army there, he opened the action, commanding all to shoot with their bows against the parapet. The Romans, meanwhile, in defending themselves, made use of their engines of war and all their bows. At first, then, the Persians did the Romans little harm, although they were shooting their arrows thick and fast, while at the same time they suffered severely at the hands of the Romans, since they were being shot at from an elevation. But later on (since it was fated that Petra be captured by Chosroes), John by some chance was shot in the neck and died, and as a result of this the other Romans ceased to care for anything. Then indeed the barbarians withdrew to their camp; for it was already growing dark; but on the following day they planned to assail the fortifications by an excavation, as follows.

The city of Petra is on one side inaccessible on account of the sea, and on the other on account of the sheer cliffs which rise there on every hand; indeed it is from this circumstance that the city has received the name it bears. And it has only one approach on the level ground, and that not very broad; for exceedingly high cliffs overhang it on either side. At that point those who formerly built the city provided that that portion of the wall should not be open to attack by making long walls which ran along beside either cliff and guarded the approach for a great distance. And they built two towers, one in each of these walls, not following the customary plan, but as follows. They refused to allow the space in the middle of the structure to be empty, but constructed the entire towers from the ground up to a great height of very large stones which fitted together, in order that they might never be shaken down by a ram or any other engine. Such, then, are the fortifications of Petra. But the Persians secretly made a tunnel into the earth and got under one of the two towers, and from there carried out many of the stones and in their place put wood, which a little later they burned. And the flame, rising little by little, weakened the stones, and all of a sudden shook the whole tower violently and straightway brought it down to the ground. And the Romans who were on the tower perceived what was being done in sufficient time so that they did not fall with it to the ground, but they fled and got inside the city wall. And now it was possible for the enemy to storm the wall from the level, and thus with no trouble to take the city by force. The Romans, therefore, in terror, opened negotiations with the barbarians, and receiving from Chosroes pledges concerning their lives and their property, they surrendered to him both themselves and the city. [541 A.D.] Thus Chosroes captured Petra. And finding the treasures of John, which were extremely rich, he took them himself, but besides this neither he himself nor anyone else of the Persians touched anything, and the Romans, retaining their own possessions, mingled with the Median army.

XVIII

Meantime Belisarius and the Roman army, having learned nothing of what was being done there, were going in excellent order from the city of Daras toward Nisibis. And when they had reached the middle of their journey, Belisarius led the army to the right where there were abundant springs of water and level ground sufficient for all to camp upon. And there he gave orders to make a camp at about forty-two stades from the city of Nisibis. But all the others marvelled greatly that he did not wish to camp close to the fortifications, and some were quite unwilling to follow him. Belisarius therefore addressed those of the officers who were about him thus: "It was not my wish to disclose to all what I am thinking. For talk carried about through a camp cannot keep secrets, for it advances little by little until it is carried out even to the enemy. But seeing that the majority of you are allowing yourselves to act in a most disorderly manner, and that each one wishes to be himself supreme commander in the war, I shall now say among you things about which one ought to keep silence, mentioning, however, this first, that when many in an army follow independent judgments it is impossible that anything needful be done. Now I think that Chosroes, in going against other barbarians, has by no means left his own land without sufficient protection, and in particular this city which is of the first rank and is set as a defence to his whole land. In this city I know well that he has stationed soldiers in such number and of such valour as to be sufficient to stand in the way of our assaults. And the proof of this you have near at hand. For he put in command of these men the general Nabedes, who, after Chosroes himself at least, seems to be first among the Persians in glory and in every other sort of honour. This man, I believe, will both make trial of our strength and will permit of our passing by on no other condition than that he be defeated by us in battle. If, therefore, the conflict should be close by the city, the struggle will not be even for us and the Persians. For they, coming out from their stronghold against us, in case of success, should it so happen, will feel unlimited confidence in assailing us, and in case of defeat they will easily escape from our attack. For we shall only be able to pursue them a short distance, and from this no harm will come to the city, which you surely see cannot be captured by storming the wall when soldiers are defending it. But if the enemy engage with us here and we conquer them, I have great hopes, fellow officers, of capturing the city. For while our antagonists are fleeing a long way, we shall either mingle with them and rush inside the gates with them, as is probable, or we shall anticipate them and compel them to turn and escape to some other place, and thus render Nisibis without its defenders easy of capture for us."

When Belisarius had said this, all the others except Peter were convinced, and they made camp and remained with him. He, however, associating with himself John, who commanded the troops in Mesopotamia and had no small part of the army, came up to a position not far removed from the fortifications, about ten stades away, and remained quietly there. But Belisarius marshalled the men who were with him as if for combat, and sent word to Peter and his men also to hold themselves in array for battle, until he himself should give the signal; and he said that he knew well that the barbarians would attack them about midday, remembering, as they surely would, that while they themselves are accustomed to partake of food in the late afternoon, the Romans do so about midday. So Belisarius gave this warning; but Peter and his men disregarded his commands, and about midday, being distressed by the sun (for the place is exceedingly dry and hot), they stacked their arms, and with never a thought of the enemy began to go about in disorderly fashion and eat gourds which grew there. And when this was observed by Nabedes, he led the Persian army running at full speed against them. And the Romans, since they did not fail to observe that the Persians were coming out of the fortifications (for they were seen clearly because moving over a level plain), sent to Belisarius urging him to support them, and they themselves snatched up their arms, and in disorder and confusion confronted their foe. But Belisarius and his men, even before the messenger had reached them, discovered by the dust the attack of the Persians, and went to the rescue on the run. And when the Persians came up, the Romans did not withstand their onset, but were routed without any difficulty, and the Persians, following close upon them, killed fifty men, and seized and kept the standard of Peter. And they would have slain them all in this pursuit, for the Romans had no thought of resistance, if Belisarius and the army with him had not come upon them and prevented it. For as the Goths, first of all, came upon them with long spears in close array, the Persians did not await their attack but beat a hasty retreat. And the Romans together with the Goths followed them up and slew a hundred and fifty men. For the pursuit was only of short duration, and the others quickly got inside the fortifications. Then indeed all the Romans withdrew to the camp of Belisarius, and the Persians on the following day set up on a tower instead of a trophy the standard of Peter, and hanging sausages from it they taunted the enemy with laughter; however, they no longer dared to come out against them, but they guarded the city securely.

And Belisarius, seeing that Nisibis was exceedingly strong, and having no hope regarding its capture, was eager to go forward, in order that he might do the enemy some damage by a sudden inroad. Accordingly he broke camp and moved forward with the whole army. And after accomplishing a day's journey, they came upon a fortress which the Persians call Sisauranon. There were in that place besides the numerous population eight hundred horsemen, the best of the Persians, who were keeping guard under command of a man of note, Bleschames by name. And the Romans made camp close by the fortress and began a siege, but, upon making an assault upon the fortifications, they were beaten back, losing many men in the fight. For the wall happened to be extremely strong, and the barbarians defended it against their assailants with the greatest vigour. Belisarius therefore called together all the officers and spoke as follows: "Experience in many wars, fellow officers, has made it possible for us in difficult situations to foresee what will come to pass, and has made us capable of avoiding disaster by choosing the better course. You understand, therefore, how great a mistake it is for an army to proceed into a hostile land, when many strongholds and many fighting men in them have been left in the rear. Now exactly this has happened to us in the present case. For if we continue our advance, some of the enemy from this place as well as from the city of Nisibis will follow us secretly and will, in all probability, handle us roughly in places which are for them conveniently adapted for an ambuscade or some other sort of attack. And if, by any chance, a second army confronts us and opens battle, it will be necessary for us to array ourselves against both, and we should thus suffer irreparable harm at their hands. And in saying this I do not mention the fact that if we fail in the engagement, should it so happen, we shall after that have absolutely no way of return left to the land of the Romans. Let us not therefore by reason of most ill-considered haste seem to have been our own despoilers, nor by our eagerness for strife do harm to the cause of the Romans. For stupid daring leads to destruction, but discreet hesitation is well adapted always to save those who adopt such a course. Let us therefore establish ourselves here and endeavour to capture this fortress, and let Arethas with his forces be sent into the country of Assyria. For the Saracens are by nature unable to storm a wall, but the cleverest of all men at plundering. And some of the soldiers who are good fighters will join them in the invasion, so that, if no opposition presents itself to them, they may overwhelm those who fall in their way, and if any hostile force encounters them, they may be saved easily by retiring to us. And after we have captured the fortress, if God wills, then with the whole army let us cross the River Tigris, without having to fear mischief from anyone in our rear, and knowing well how matters stand with the Assyrians."

These words of Belisarius seemed to all well spoken, and he straightway put the plan into execution. Accordingly he commanded Arethas with his troops to advance into Assyria, and with them he sent twelve hundred soldiers, the most of whom were from among his own guard, putting two guardsmen in command of them, Trajan and John who was called the Glutton, both capable warriors. These men he directed to obey Arethas in everything they did, and he commanded Arethas to pillage all that lay before him and then return to the camp and report how matters stood with the Assyrians with regard to military strength. So Arethas and his men crossed the River Tigris and entered Assyria. There they found a goodly land and one which had been free from plunder for a long time, and undefended besides; and moving rapidly they pillaged many of the places there and secured a great amount of rich plunder. And at that time Belisarius captured some of the Persians and learned from them that those who were inside the fortress were altogether out of provisions. For they do not observe the custom which is followed in the cities of Daras and Nisibis, where they put away the annual food-supply in public store-houses, and now that a hostile army had fallen upon them unexpectedly they had not anticipated the event by carrying in any of the necessities of life. And since a great number of persons had taken refuge suddenly in the fortress, they were naturally hard pressed by the want of provisions. When Belisarius learned this, he sent George, a man of the greatest discretion with whom he shared his secrets, to test the men of the place, in the hope that he might be able to arrange some terms of surrender and thus take the place. And George succeeded, after addressing to them many words of exhortation and of kindly invitation, in persuading them to take pledges for their safety and to deliver themselves and the fortress to the Romans. Thus Belisarius captured Sisauranon, and the inhabitants, all of whom were Christians and of Roman origin, he released unscathed, but the Persians he sent with Bleschames to Byzantium, and razed the fortification wall of the fortress to the ground. And the emperor not long afterwards sent these Persians and Bleschames to Italy to fight against the Goths. Such, then, was the course of events which had to do with the fortress of Sisauranon.

But Arethas, fearing lest he should be despoiled of his booty by the Romans, was now unwilling to return to the camp. So he sent some of his followers ostensibly for the purpose of reconnoitring, but secretly commanding them to return as quickly as possible and announce to the army that a large hostile force was at the crossing of the river. For this reason, then, he advised Trajan and John to return by another route to the land of the Romans. So they did not come again to Belisarius, but keeping the River Euphrates on the right they finally arrived at the Theodosiopolis which is near the River Aborrhas. But Belisarius and the Roman army, hearing nothing concerning this force, were disturbed, and they were filled with fear and an intolerable and exaggerated suspicion. And since much time had been consumed by them in this siege, it came about that many of the soldiers were taken there with a troublesome fever; for the portion of Mesopotamia which is subject to the Persians is extremely dry and hot. And the Romans were not accustomed to this and especially those who came from Thrace; and since they were living their daily life in a place where the heat was excessive and in stuffy huts in the summer season, they became so ill that the third part of the army were lying half-dead. The whole army, therefore, was eager to depart from there and return as quickly as possible to their own land, and most of all the commanders of the troops in Lebanon, Rhecithancus and Theoctistus, who saw that the time which was the sacred season of the Saracens had in fact already passed. They came, indeed, frequently to Belisarius and entreated him to release them immediately, protesting that they had given over to Alamoundaras the country of Lebanon and Syria, and were sitting there for no good reason.

Belisarius therefore called together all the officers and opened a discussion. Then John, the son of Nicetas, rose first and spoke as follows: "Most excellent Belisarius, I consider that in all time there has never been a general such as you are either in fortune or in valour. And this reputation has come to prevail not alone among the Romans, but also among all barbarians. This fair name, however, you will preserve most securely, if you should be able to take us back alive to the land of the Romans; for now indeed the hopes which we may have are not bright. For I would have you look thus at the situation of this army. The Saracens and the most efficient soldiers of the army crossed the River Tigris, and one day, I know not how long since, they found themselves in such a plight that they have not even succeeded in sending a messenger to us, and Rhecithancus and Theoctistus will depart, as you see surely, believing that the army of Alamoundaras is almost at this very moment in the midst of Phoenicia, pillaging the whole country there. And among those who are left the sick are so numerous that those who will care for them and convey them to the land of the Romans are fewer in number than they are by a great deal. Under these circumstances, if it should fall out that any hostile force should come upon us, either while remaining here or while going back, not a man would be able to carry back word to the Romans in Daras of the calamity which had befallen us. For as for going forward, I consider it impossible even to be spoken of. While, therefore, some hope is still left, it will be of advantage both to make plans for the return and to put the plans into action. For when men have come into danger and especially such danger as this, it is downright folly for them to devote their thoughts not to safety, but to opposition to the enemy." So spoke John, and all the others expressed approval, and becoming disorderly, they demanded that the retreat be made with all speed. Accordingly Belisarius laid the sick in the carts and let them lead the way, while he led the army behind them. And as soon as they got into the land of the Romans, he learned everything which had been done by Arethas, but he did not succeed in inflicting any punishment upon him, for he never came into his sight again. So ended the invasion of the Romans.

And after Chosroes had taken Petra, it was announced to him that Belisarius had invaded the Persian territory, and the engagement near the city of Nisibis was reported, as also the capture of the fortress of Sisauranon, and all that the army of Arethas had done after crossing the River Tigris. Straightway, then, he established a garrison in Petra, and with the rest of the army and those of the Romans who had been captured he marched away into the land of Persia. Such, then, were the events which took place in the second invasion of Chosroes. And Belisarius went to Byzantium at the summons of the emperor, and passed the winter there.

XX

[542 A.D.] At the opening of spring Chosroes, the son of Cabades, for the third time began an invasion into the land of the Romans with a mighty army, keeping the River Euphrates on the right. And Candidus, the priest of Sergiopolis, upon learning that the Median army had come near there, began to be afraid both for himself and for the city, since he had by no means carried out at the appointed time the agreement which he had made[15]; accordingly he went into the camp of the enemy and entreated Chosroes not to be angry with him because of this. For as for money, he had never had any, and for this reason he had not even wished in the first place to deliver the inhabitants of Sura, and though he had supplicated the Emperor Justinian many times on their behalf, he had failed to receive any help from him. But Chosroes put him under guard, and, torturing him most cruelly, claimed the right to exact from him double the amount of money, just as had been agreed. And Candidus entreated him to send men to Sergiopolis to take all the treasures of the sanctuary there. And when Chosroes followed this suggestion, Candidus sent some of his followers with them. So the inhabitants of Sergiopolis, receiving into the city the men sent by Chosroes, gave them many of the treasures, declaring that nothing else was left them. But Chosroes said that these were by no means sufficient for him, and demanded that he should receive others still more than these. Accordingly he sent men, ostensibly to search out with all diligence the wealth of the city, but in reality to take possession of the city. But since it was fated that Sergiopolis should not be taken by the Persians, one of the Saracens, who, though a Christian, was serving under Alamoundaras, Ambrus by name, came by night along the wall of the city, and reporting to them the whole plan, bade them by no means receive the Persians into the city. Thus those who were sent by Chosroes returned to him unsuccessful, and he, boiling with anger, began to make plans to capture the city. He accordingly sent an army of six thousand, commanding them to begin a siege and to make assaults upon the fortifications. And this army came there and commenced active operations, and the citizens of Sergiopolis at first defended themselves vigorously, but later they gave up, and in terror at the danger, they were purposing to give over the city to the enemy. For, as it happened, they had not more than two hundred soldiers. But Ambrus, again coming along by the fortifications at night, said that within two days the Persians would raise the siege since their water supply had failed them absolutely. For this reason they did not by any means open negotiations with the enemy, and the barbarians, suffering with thirst, removed from there and came to Chosroes. However, Chosroes never released Candidus. For it was necessary, I suppose, that since he had disregarded his sworn agreement, he should be a priest no longer. Such, then, was the course of these events.

But when Chosroes arrived at the land of the Commagenae which they call Euphratesia, he had no desire to turn to plundering or to the capture of any stronghold, since he had previously taken everything before him as far as Syria, partly by capture and partly by exacting money, as has been set forth in the preceding narrative. And his purpose was to lead the army straight for Palestine, in order that he might plunder all their treasures and especially those in Jerusalem. For he had it from hearsay that this was an especially goodly land and peopled by wealthy inhabitants. And all the Romans, both officers and soldiers, were far from entertaining any thought of confronting the enemy or of standing in the way of their passage, but manning their strongholds as each one could, they thought it sufficient to preserve them and save themselves.

The Emperor Justinian, upon learning of the inroad of the Persians, again sent Belisarius against them. And he came with great speed to Euphratesia since he had no army with him, riding on the government post-horses, which they are accustomed to call "veredi," while Justus, the nephew of the emperor, together with Bouzes and certain others, was in Hierapolis where he had fled for refuge. And when these men heard that Belisarius was coming and was not far away, they wrote a letter to him which ran as follows: "Once more Chosroes, as you yourself doubtless know, has taken the field against the Romans, bringing a much greater army than formerly; and where he is purposing to go is not yet evident, except indeed that we hear he is very near, and that he has injured no place, but is always moving ahead. But come to us as quickly as possible, if indeed you are able to escape detection by the army of the enemy, in order that you yourself may be safe for the emperor, and that you may join us in guarding Hierapolis." Such was the message of the letter. But Belisarius, not approving the advice given, came to the place called Europum, which is on the River Euphrates. From there he sent about in all directions and began to gather his army, and there he established his camp; and the officers in Hierapolis he answered with the following words: "If, now, Chosroes is proceeding against any other peoples, and not against subjects of the Romans, this plan of yours is well considered and insures the greatest possible degree of safety; for it is great folly for those who have the opportunity of remaining quiet and being rid of trouble to enter into any unnecessary danger; but if, immediately after departing from here, this barbarian is going to fall upon some other territory of the Emperor Justinian, and that an exceptionally good one, but without any guard of soldiers, be assured that to perish valorously is better in every way than to be saved without a fight. For this would justly be called not salvation but treason. But come as quickly as possible to Europum, where, after collecting the whole army, I hope to deal with the enemy as God permits." And when the officers saw this message, they took courage, and leaving there Justus with some few men in order to guard Hierapolis, all the others with the rest of the army came to Europum.

XXI

But Chosroes, upon learning that Belisarius with the whole Roman army had encamped at Europum, decided not to continue his advance, but sent one of the royal secretaries, Abandanes by name, a man who enjoyed a great reputation for discretion, to Belisarius, in order to find out by inspection what sort of a general he might be, but ostensibly to make a protest because the Emperor Justinian had not sent the ambassadors to the Persians at all in order that they might settle the arrangements for the peace as had been agreed. When Belisarius learned this, he did as follows. He himself picked out six thousand men of goodly stature and especially fine physique, and set out to hunt at a considerable distance from the camp. Then he commanded Diogenes, the guardsman, and Adolius, the son of Acacius, to cross the river with a thousand horsemen and to move about the bank there, always making it appear to the enemy that if they wished to cross the Euphrates and proceed to their own land, they would never permit them to do so. This Adolius was an Armenian by birth, and he always served the emperor while in the palace as privy counsellor (those who enjoy this honour are called by the Romans "silentiarii"), but at that time he was commander of some Armenians. And these men did as directed.

Now when Belisarius had ascertained that the envoy was close at hand, he set up a tent of some heavy cloth, of the sort which is commonly called a "pavilion," and seated himself there as one might in a desolate place, seeking thus to indicate that he had come without any equipment. And he arranged the soldiers as follows. On either side of the tent were Thracians and Illyrians, with Goths beyond them, and next to these Eruli, and finally Vandals and Moors. And their line extended for a great distance over the plain. For they did not remain standing always in the same place, but stood apart from one another and kept walking about, looking carelessly and without the least interest upon the envoy of Chosroes. And not one of them had a cloak or any other outer garment to cover the shoulders, but they were sauntering about clad in linen tunics and trousers, and outside these their girdles. And each one had his horse-whip, but for weapons one had a sword, another an axe, another an uncovered bow. And all gave the impression that they were eager to be off on the hunt with never a thought of anything else. So Abandanes came into the presence of Belisarius and said that the king Chosroes was indignant because the agreement previously made had not been kept, in that the envoys had not been sent to him by Caesar (for thus the Persians call the emperor of the Romans), and as a result of this Chosroes had been compelled to come into the land of the Romans in arms. But Belisarius was not terrified by the thought that such a multitude of barbarians were encamped close by, nor did he experience any confusion because of the words of the man, but with a laughing, care-free countenance he made answer, saying: "This course which Chosroes has followed on the present occasion is not in keeping with the way men usually act. For other men, in case a dispute should arise between themselves and any of their neighbours, first carry on negotiations with them, and whenever they do not receive reasonable satisfaction, then finally go against them in war. But he first comes into the midst of the Romans, and then begins to offer suggestions concerning peace." With such words as these he dismissed the ambassador.

And when Abandanes came to Chosroes, he advised him to take his departure with all possible speed. For he said he had met a general who in manliness and sagacity surpassed all other men, and soldiers such as he at least had never seen, whose orderly conduct had roused in him the greatest admiration. And he added that the contest was not on an even footing as regards risk for him and for Belisarius, for there was this difference, that if he conquered, he himself would conquer the slave of Caesar, but if he by any chance were defeated, he would bring great disgrace upon his kingdom and upon the race of the Persians; and again the Romans, if conquered, could easily save themselves in strongholds and in their own land, while if the Persians should meet with any reverse, not even a messenger would escape to the land of the Persians. Chosroes was convinced by this admonition and wished to turn back to his own country, but he found himself in a very perplexing situation. For he supposed that the crossing of the river was being guarded by the enemy, and he was unable to march back by the same road, which was entirely destitute of human habitation, since the supplies which they had at the first when they invaded the land of the Romans had already entirely failed them. At last after long consideration it seemed to him most advantageous to risk a battle and get to the opposite side, and to make the journey through a land abounding in all good things. Now Belisarius knew well that not even a hundred thousand men would ever be sufficient to check the crossing of Chosroes. For the river at many places along there can be crossed in boats very easily, and even apart from this the Persian army was too strong to be excluded from the crossing by an enemy numerically insignificant. But he had at first commanded the troops of Diogenes and Adolius, together with the thousand horsemen, to move about the bank at that point in order to confuse the barbarian by a feeling of helplessness. But after frightening this same barbarian, as I have said, Belisarius feared lest there should be some obstacle in the way of his departing from the land of the Romans. For it seemed to him a most significant achievement to have driven away from there the army of Chosroes, without risking any battle against so many myriads of barbarians with soldiers who were very few in number and who were in abject terror of the Median army. For this reason he commanded Diogenes and Adolius to remain quiet.

Chosroes, accordingly, constructed a bridge with great celerity and crossed the River Euphrates suddenly with his whole army. For the Persians are able to cross all rivers without the slightest difficulty because when they are on the march they have in readiness hook-shaped irons with which they fasten together long timbers, and with the help of these they improvise a bridge on the spur of the moment wherever they may desire. And as soon as he had reached the land on the opposite side, he sent to Belisarius and said that he, for his part, had bestowed a favour upon the Romans in the withdrawal of the Median army, and that he was expecting the envoys from them, who ought to present themselves to him at no distant time. Then Belisarius also with the whole Roman army crossed the River Euphrates and immediately sent to Chosroes. And when the messengers came into his presence, they commended him highly for his withdrawal and promised that envoys would come to him promptly from the emperor, who would arrange with him that the terms which had previously been agreed upon concerning the peace should be put into effect. And they asked of him that he treat the Romans as his friends in his journey through their land. This too he agreed to carry out, if they should give him some one of their notable men as a hostage to make this compact binding, in order that they might carry out their agreement. So the envoys returned to Belisarius and reported the words of Chosroes, and he came to Edessa and chose John, the son of Basilius, the most illustrious of all the inhabitants of Edessa in birth and in wealth, and straightway sent him, much against his will, as a hostage to Chosroes. And the Romans were loud in their praises of Belisarius and he seemed to have achieved greater glory in their eyes by this affair than when he brought Gelimer or Vittigis captive to Byzantium. For in reality it was an achievement of great importance and one deserving great praise, that, at a time when all the Romans were panic-stricken with fear and were hiding themselves in their defences, and Chosroes with a mighty army had come into the midst of the Roman domain, a general with only a few men, coming in hot haste from Byzantium just at that moment, should have set his camp over against that of the Persian king, and that Chosroes unexpectedly, either through fear of fortune or of the valour of the man or even because deceived by some tricks, should no longer continue his advance, but should in reality take to flight, though pretending to be seeking peace.

But in the meantime Chosroes, disregarding the agreement, took the city of Callinicus which was entirely without defenders. For the Romans, seeing that the wall of this city was altogether unsound and easy of capture, were tearing down portions of it in turn and restoring them with new construction. Now just at that time they had torn down one section of it and had not yet built in this interval; when, therefore, they learned that the enemy were close at hand, they carried out the most precious of their treasures, and the wealthy inhabitants withdrew to other strongholds, while the rest without soldiers remained where they were. And it happened that great numbers of farmers had gathered there. These Chosroes enslaved and razed everything to the ground. A little later, upon receiving the hostage, John, he retired to his own country. And the Armenians who had submitted to Chosroes received pledges from the Romans and came with Bassaces to Byzantium. Such was the fortune of the Romans in the third invasion of Chosroes. And Belisarius came to Byzantium at the summons of the emperor, in order to be sent again to Italy, since the situation there was already full of difficulties for the Romans.

XXII

[542 A.D.] During these times there was a pestilence, by which the whole human race came near to being annihilated. Now in the case of all other scourges sent from Heaven some explanation of a cause might be given by daring men, such as the many theories propounded by those who are clever in these matters; for they love to conjure up causes which are absolutely incomprehensible to man, and to fabricate outlandish theories of natural philosophy, knowing well that they are saying nothing sound, but considering it sufficient for them, if they completely deceive by their argument some of those whom they meet and persuade them to their view. But for this calamity it is quite impossible either to express in words or to conceive in thought any explanation, except indeed to refer it to God. For it did not come in a part of the world nor upon certain men, nor did it confine itself to any season of the year, so that from such circumstances it might be possible to find subtle explanations of a cause, but it embraced the entire world, and blighted the lives of all men, though differing from one another in the most marked degree, respecting neither sex nor age. For much as men differ with regard to places in which they live, or in the law of their daily life, or in natural bent, or in active pursuits, or in whatever else man differs from man, in the case of this disease alone the difference availed naught. And it attacked some in the summer season, others in the winter, and still others at the other times of the year. Now let each one express his own judgment concerning the matter, both sophist and astrologer, but as for me, I shall proceed to tell where this disease originated and the manner in which it destroyed men.

It started from the Aegyptians who dwell in Pelusium. Then it divided and moved in one direction towards Alexandria and the rest of Aegypt, and in the other direction it came to Palestine on the borders of Aegypt; and from there it spread over the whole world, always moving forward and travelling at times favourable to it. For it seemed to move by fixed arrangement, and to tarry for a specified time in each country, casting its blight slightingly upon none, but spreading in either direction right out to the ends of the world, as if fearing lest some corner of the earth might escape it. For it left neither island nor cave nor mountain ridge which had human inhabitants; and if it had passed by any land, either not affecting the men there or touching them in indifferent fashion, still at a later time it came back; then those who dwelt round about this land, whom formerly it had afflicted most sorely, it did not touch at all, but it did not remove from the place in question until it had given up its just and proper tale of dead, so as to correspond exactly to the number destroyed at the earlier time among those who dwelt round about. And this disease always took its start from the coast, and from there went up to the interior. And in the second year it reached Byzantium in the middle of spring, where it happened that I was staying at that time. And it came as follows. Apparitions of supernatural beings in human guise of every description were seen by many persons, and those who encountered them thought that they were struck by the man they had met in this or that part of the body, as it happened, and immediately upon seeing this apparition they were seized also by the disease. Now at first those who met these creatures tried to turn them aside by uttering the holiest of names and exorcising them in other ways as well as each one could, but they accomplished absolutely nothing, for even in the sanctuaries where the most of them fled for refuge they were dying constantly. But later on they were unwilling even to give heed to their friends when they called to them, and they shut themselves up in their rooms and pretended that they did not hear, although their doors were being beaten down, fearing, obviously, that he who was calling was one of those demons. But in the case of some the pestilence did not come on in this way, but they saw a vision in a dream and seemed to suffer the very same thing at the hands of the creature who stood over them, or else to hear a voice foretelling to them that they were written down in the number of those who were to die. But with the majority it came about that they were seized by the disease without becoming aware of what was coming either through a waking vision or a dream. And they were taken in the following manner. They had a sudden fever, some when just roused from sleep, others while walking about, and others while otherwise engaged, without any regard to what they were doing. And the body shewed no change from its previous colour, nor was it hot as might be expected when attacked by a fever, nor indeed did any inflammation set in, but the fever was of such a languid sort from its commencement and up till evening that neither to the sick themselves nor to a physician who touched them would it afford any suspicion of danger. It was natural, therefore, that not one of those who had contracted the disease expected to die from it. But on the same day in some cases, in others on the following day, and in the rest not many days later, a bubonic swelling developed; and this took place not only in the particular part of the body which is called "boubon,"[16] that is, below the abdomen, but also inside the armpit, and in some cases also beside the ears, and at different points on the thighs.

Up to this point, then, everything went in about the same way with all who had taken the disease. But from then on very marked differences developed; and I am unable to say whether the cause of this diversity of symptoms was to be found in the difference in bodies, or in the fact that it followed the wish of Him who brought the disease into the world. For there ensued with some a deep coma, with others a violent delirium, and in either case they suffered the characteristic symptoms of the disease. For those who were under the spell of the coma forgot all those who were familiar to them and seemed to be sleeping constantly. And if anyone cared for them, they would eat without waking, but some also were neglected, and these would die directly through lack of sustenance. But those who were seized with delirium suffered from insomnia and were victims of a distorted imagination; for they suspected that men were coming upon them to destroy them, and they would become excited and rush off in flight, crying out at the top of their voices. And those who were attending them were in a state of constant exhaustion and had a most difficult time of it throughout. For this reason everybody pitied them no less than the sufferers, not because they were threatened by the pestilence in going near it (for neither physicians nor other persons were found to contract this malady through contact with the sick or with the dead, for many who were constantly engaged either in burying or in attending those in no way connected with them held out in the performance of this service beyond all expectation, while with many others the disease came on without warning and they died straightway); but they pitied them because of the great hardships which they were undergoing. For when the patients fell from their beds and lay rolling upon the floor, they, kept patting them back in place, and when they were struggling to rush headlong out of their houses, they would force them back by shoving and pulling against them. And when water chanced to be near, they wished to fall into it, not so much because of a desire for drink (for the most of them rushed into the sea), but the cause was to be found chiefly in the diseased state of their minds. They had also great difficulty in the matter of eating, for they could not easily take food. And many perished through lack of any man to care for them, for they were either overcome by hunger, or threw themselves down from a height. And in those cases where neither coma nor delirium came on, the bubonic swelling became mortified and the sufferer, no longer able to endure the pain, died. And one would suppose that in all cases the same thing would have been true, but since they were not at all in their senses, some were quite unable to feel the pain; for owing to the troubled condition of their minds they lost all sense of feeling.

Now some of the physicians who were at a loss because the symptoms were not understood, supposing that the disease centred in the bubonic swellings, decided to investigate the bodies of the dead. And upon opening some of the swellings, they found a strange sort of carbuncle that had grown inside them.

Death came in some cases immediately, in others after many days; and with some the body broke out with black pustules about as large as a lentil and these did not survive even one day, but all succumbed immediately. With many also a vomiting of blood ensued without visible cause and straightway brought death. Moreover I am able to declare this, that the most illustrious physicians predicted that many would die, who unexpectedly escaped entirely from suffering shortly afterwards, and that they declared that many would be saved, who were destined to be carried off almost immediately. So it was that in this disease there was no cause which came within the province of human reasoning; for in all cases the issue tended to be something unaccountable. For example, while some were helped by bathing, others were harmed in no less degree. And of those who received no care many died, but others, contrary to reason, were saved. And again, methods of treatment shewed different results with different patients. Indeed the whole matter may be stated thus, that no device was discovered by man to save himself, so that either by taking precautions he should not suffer, or that when the malady had assailed him he should get the better of it; but suffering came without warning and recovery was due to no external cause.

And in the case of women who were pregnant death could be certainly foreseen if they were taken with the disease. For some died through miscarriage, but others perished immediately at the time of birth with the infants they bore. However, they say that three women in confinement survived though their children perished, and that one woman died at the very time of child-birth but that the child was born and survived.

Now in those cases where the swelling rose to an unusual size and a discharge of pus had set in, it came about that they escaped from the disease and survived, for clearly the acute condition of the carbuncle had found relief in this direction, and this proved to be in general an indication of returning health; but in cases where the swelling preserved its former appearance there ensued those troubles which I have just mentioned. And with some of them it came about that the thigh was withered, in which case, though the swelling was there, it did not develop the least suppuration. With others who survived the tongue did not remain unaffected, and they lived on either lisping or speaking incoherently and with difficulty.

XXIII

Now the disease in Byzantium ran a course of four months, and its greatest virulence lasted about three. And at first the deaths were a little more than the normal, then the mortality rose still higher, and afterwards the tale of dead reached five thousand each day, and again it even came to ten thousand and still more than that. Now in the beginning each man attended to the burial of the dead of his own house, and these they threw even into the tombs of others, either escaping detection or using violence; but afterwards confusion and disorder everywhere became complete. For slaves remained destitute of masters, and men who in former times were very prosperous were deprived of the service of their domestics who were either sick or dead, and many houses became completely destitute of human inhabitants. For this reason it came about that some of the notable men of the city because of the universal destitution remained unburied for many days.

And it fell to the lot of the emperor, as was natural, to make provision for the trouble. He therefore detailed soldiers from the palace and distributed money, commanding Theodorus to take charge of this work; this man held the position of announcer of imperial messages, always announcing to the emperor the petitions of his clients, and declaring to them in turn whatever his wish was. In the Latin tongue the Romans designate this office by the term "referendarius." So those who had not as yet fallen into complete destitution in their domestic affairs attended individually to the burial of those connected with them. But Theodorus, by giving out the emperor's money and by making further expenditures from his own purse, kept burying the bodies which were not cared for. And when it came about that all the tombs which had existed previously were filled with the dead, then they dug up all the places about the city one after the other, laid the dead there, each one as he could, and departed; but later on those who were making these trenches, no longer able to keep up with the number of the dying, mounted the towers of the fortifications in Sycae[17], and tearing off the roofs threw the bodies in there in complete disorder; and they piled them up just as each one happened to fall, and filled practically all the towers with corpses, and then covered them again with their roofs. As a result of this an evil stench pervaded the city and distressed the inhabitants still more, and especially whenever the wind blew fresh from that quarter.

At that time all the customary rites of burial were overlooked. For the dead were not carried out escorted by a procession in the customary manner, nor were the usual chants sung over them, but it was sufficient if one carried on his shoulders the body of one of the dead to the parts of the city which bordered on the sea and flung him down; and there the corpses would be thrown upon skiffs in a heap, to be conveyed wherever it might chance. At that time, too, those of the population who had formerly been members of the factions laid aside their mutual enmity and in common they attended to the burial rites of the dead, and they carried with their own hands the bodies of those who were no connections of theirs and buried them. Nay, more, those who in times past used to take delight in devoting themselves to pursuits both shameful and base, shook off the unrighteousness of their daily lives and practised the duties of religion with diligence, not so much because they had learned wisdom at last nor because they had become all of a sudden lovers of virtue, as it were, for when qualities have become fixed in men by nature or by the training of a long period of time, it is impossible for them to lay them aside thus lightly, except, indeed, some divine influence for good has breathed upon them but then all, so to speak, being thoroughly terrified by the things which were happening, and supposing that they would die immediately, did, as was natural, learn respectability for a season by sheer necessity. Therefore as soon as they were rid of the disease and were saved, and already supposed that they were in security, since the curse had moved on to other peoples, then they turned sharply about and reverted once more to their baseness of heart, and now, more than before, they make a display of the inconsistency of their conduct, altogether surpassing themselves in villainy and in lawlessness of every sort. For one could insist emphatically without falsehood that this disease, whether by chance or by some providence, chose out with exactitude the worst men and let them go free. But these things were displayed to the world in later times.

During that time it seemed no easy thing to see any man in the streets of Byzantium, but all who had the good fortune to be in health were sitting in their houses, either attending the sick or mourning the dead. And if one did succeed in meeting a man going out, he was carrying one of the dead. And work of every description ceased, and all the trades were abandoned by the artisans, and all other work as well, such as each had in hand. Indeed in a city which was simply abounding in all good things starvation almost absolute was running riot. Certainly it seemed a difficult and very notable thing to have a sufficiency of bread or of anything else; so that with some of the sick it appeared that the end of life came about sooner than it should have come by reason of the lack of the necessities of life. And, to put all in a word, it was not possible to see a single man in Byzantium clad in the chlamys[18], and especially when the emperor became ill (for he too had a swelling of the groin), but in a city which held dominion over the whole Roman empire every man was wearing clothes befitting private station and remaining quietly at home. Such was the course of the pestilence in the Roman empire at large as well as in Byzantium. And it fell also upon the land of the Persians and visited all the other barbarians besides.

XXIV

[545 A.D.] Now it happened that Chosroes had come from Assyria to a place toward the north called Adarbiganon, from which he was planning to make an invasion into the Roman domain through Persarmenia. In that place is the great sanctuary of fire, which the Persians reverence above all other gods. There the fire is guarded unquenched by the Magi, and they perform carefully a great number of sacred rites, and in particular they consult an oracle on those matters which are of the greatest importance. This is the fire which the Romans worshipped under the name of Hestia[19] in ancient times. There someone who had been sent from Byzantium to Chosroes announced that Constantianus and Sergius would come before him directly as envoys to arrange the treaty. Now these two men were both trained speakers and exceedingly clever; Constantianus was an Illyrian by birth, and Sergius was from the city of Edessa in Mesopotamia. And Chosroes remained quiet expecting these men. But in the course of the journey thither Constantianus became ill and much time was consumed; in the meantime it came about that the pestilence fell upon the Persians. For this reason Nabedes, who at that time held the office of general in Persarmenia, sent the priest of the Christians in Dubios by direction of the king to Valerianus, the general in Armenia, in order to reproach the envoys for their tardiness and to urge the Romans with all zeal toward peace. And he came with his brother to Armenia, and, meeting Valerianus, declared that he himself, as a Christian, was favourably disposed toward the Romans, and that the king Chosroes always followed his advice in every matter; so that if the ambassadors would come with him to the land of Persia, there would be nothing to prevent them from arranging the peace as they wished. Thus then spoke the priest; but the brother of the priest met Valerianus secretly and said that Chosroes was in great straits: for his son had risen against him in an attempt to set up a tyranny, and he himself together with the whole Persian army had been taken with the plague; and this was the reason why he wished just now to settle the agreement with the Romans. When Valerianus heard this, he straightway dismissed the bishop, promising that the envoys would come to Chosroes at no distant time, but he himself reported the words which he had heard to the Emperor Justinian. This led the emperor immediately to send word to him and to Martinus and the other commanders to invade the enemy's territory as quickly as possible. For he knew well that no one of the enemy would stand in their way. And he commanded them to gather all in one place and so make their invasion into Persarmenia. When the commanders received these letters, all of them together with their followers began to gather into the land of Armenia.

And already Chosroes had abandoned Adarbiganon a little before through fear of the plague and was off with his whole army into Assyria, where the pestilence had not as yet become epidemic. Valerianus accordingly encamped close by Theodosiopolis with the troops under him; and with him was arrayed Narses, who had with him Armenians and some of the Eruli. And Martinus, the General of the East, together with Ildiger and Theoctistus, reached the fortress of Citharizon, and fixing his camp there, remained on the spot. This fortress is separated from Theodosiopolis by a journey of four days. There too Peter came not long afterwards together with Adolius and some other commanders. Now the troops in this region were commanded by Isaac, the brother of Narses. And Philemouth and Beros with the Eruli who were under them came into the territory of Chorzianene, not far from the camp of Martinus. And Justus, the emperor's nephew, and Peranius and John, the son of Nicetas, together with Domentiolus and John, who was called the Glutton, made camp near the place called Phison, which is close by the boundaries of Martyropolis. Thus then were encamped the Roman commanders with their troops; and the whole army amounted to thirty thousand men. Now all these troops were neither gathered into one place, nor indeed was there any general meeting for conference. But the generals sent to each other some of their followers and began to make enquiries concerning the invasion. Suddenly, however, Peter, without communicating with anyone, and without any careful consideration, invaded the hostile land with his troops. And when on the following day this was found out by Philemouth and Beros, the leaders of the Eruli, they straightway followed. And when this in turn came to the knowledge of Martinus and Valerianus and their men, they quickly joined in the invasion. And all of them a little later united with each other in the enemy's territory, with the exception of Justus and his men, who, as I have said, had encamped far away from the rest of the army, and learned later of their invasion; then, indeed, they also invaded the territory of the enemy as quickly as possible at the point where they were, but failed altogether to unite with the other commanders. As for the others, they proceeded in a body straight for Doubios, neither plundering nor damaging in any other way the land of the Persians.

XXV

Now Doubios is a land excellent in every respect, and especially blessed with a healthy climate and abundance of good water; and from Theodosiopolis it is removed a journey of eight days. In that region there are plains suitable for riding, and many very populous villages are situated in very close proximity to one another, and numerous merchants conduct their business in them. For from India and the neighbouring regions of Iberia and from practically all the nations of Persia and some of those under Roman sway they bring in merchandise and carry on their dealings with each other there. And the priest of the Christians is called "Catholicos" in the Greek tongue, because he presides alone over the whole region. Now at a distance of about one hundred and twenty stades from Doubios on the right as one travels from the land of the Romans, there is a mountain difficult of ascent and moreover precipitous, and a village crowded into very narrow space by the rough country about, Anglon by name. Thither Nabedes withdrew with his whole army as soon as he learned of the inroad of the enemy, and, confident in his strength of position, he shut himself in. Now the village lies at the extremity of the mountain, and there is a strong fortress bearing the same name as this village on the steep mountain side. So Nabedes with stones and carts blocked up the entrances into the village and thus made it still more difficult of access. And in front of it he dug a sort of trench and stationed the army there, having filled some old cabins with ambuscades of infantrymen Altogether the Persian army amounted to four thousand men.

While these things were being done in this way, the Romans reached a place one day's journey distant from Anglon, and capturing one of the enemy who was going out as a spy they enquired where in the world Nabedes was then. And he asserted that the man had retired from Anglon with the whole Median army. And when Narses heard this, he was indignant, and he heaped reproaches and abuse upon his fellow-commanders for their hesitation. And others, too, began to do the very same thing, casting insults upon one another; and from then on, giving up all thought of battle and danger, they were eager to plunder the country thereabout. The troops broke camp, accordingly, and without the guidance of generals and without observing any definite formation, they moved forward in complete confusion; for neither had they any countersign among themselves, as is customary in such perilous situations, nor were they arranged in their proper divisions. For the soldiers marched forward, mixed in with the baggage train, as if going to the ready plunder of great wealth. But when they came near to Anglon, they sent out spies who returned to them announcing the array of the enemy. And the generals were thunder-struck by the unexpectedness of it, but they considered it altogether disgraceful and unmanly to turn back with an army of such great size, and so they disposed the army in its three divisions, as well as the circumstances permitted, and advanced straight toward the enemy. Now Peter held the right wing and Valerianus the left, while Martinus and his men arrayed themselves in the centre. And when they came close to their opponents, they halted, preserving their formation, but not without disorder. The cause for this was to be found in the difficulty of the ground, which was very badly broken up, and in the fact that they were entering battle in a formation arranged on the spur of the moment. And up to this time the barbarians, who had gathered themselves into a small space, were remaining quiet, considering the strength of their antagonists, since the order had been given them by Nabedes not under any circumstances to begin the fighting, but if the enemy should assail them, to defend themselves with all their might.

And first Narses with the Eruli and those of the Romans who were under him, engaged with the enemy, and after a hard hand-to-hand struggle, he routed the Persians who were before him. And the barbarians in flight ascended on the run to the fortress, and in so doing they inflicted terrible injury upon one another in the narrow way. And then Narses urged his men forward and pressed still harder upon the enemy, and the rest of the Romans joined in the action. But all of a sudden the men who were in ambush, as has been said[20], came out from the cabins along the narrow alleys, and killed some of the Eruli, falling unexpectedly upon them, and they struck Narses himself a blow on the temple. And his brother Isaac carried him out from among the fighting men, mortally wounded. And he died shortly afterwards, having proved himself a brave man in this engagement. Then, as was to be expected, great confusion fell upon the Roman army, and Nabedes let out the whole Persian force upon his opponents. And the Persians, shooting into great masses of the enemy in the narrow alleys, killed a large number without difficulty, and particularly of the Eruli who had at the first fallen upon the enemy with Narses and were fighting for the most part without protection. For the Eruli have neither helmet nor corselet nor any other protective armour, except a shield and a thick jacket, which they gird about them before they enter a struggle. And indeed the Erulian slaves go into battle without even a shield, and when they prove themselves brave men in war, then their masters permit them to protect themselves in battle with shields. Such is the custom of the Eruli.

And the Romans did not withstand the enemy and all of them fled as fast as they could, never once thinking of resistance and heedless of shame or of any other worthy motive. But the Persians, suspecting that they had not turned thus to a shameless flight, but that they were making use of some ambuscades against them, pursued them as far as the rough ground extended and then turned back, not daring to fight a decisive battle on level ground, a few against many. The Romans, however, and especially all the generals, supposing that the enemy were continuing the pursuit without pause, kept fleeing still faster, wasting not a moment; and they were urging on their horses as they ran with whip and voice, and throwing their corselets and other accoutrements in haste and confusion to the ground. For they had not the courage to array themselves against the Persians if they overtook them, but they placed all hope of safety in their horses' feet, and, in short, the flight became such that scarcely any one of their horses survived, but when they stopped running, they straightway fell down and expired. And this proved a disaster for the Romans so great as to exceed anything that had ever befallen them previously. For great numbers of them perished and still more fell into the hands of the enemy. And their weapons and draught animals which were taken by the enemy amounted to such an imposing number that Persia seemed as a result of this affair to have become richer. And Adolius, while passing through a fortified place during this retreat, it was situated in Persarmenia, was struck on the head by a stone thrown by one of the inhabitants of the town, and died there. As for the forces of Justus and Peranius, they invaded the country about Taraunon, and after gathering some little plunder, immediately returned.

XXVI

[544 A.D.] And in the following year, Chosroes, the son of Cabades, for the fourth time invaded the land of the Romans, leading his army towards Mesopotamia. Now this invasion was made by this Chosroes not against Justinian, the Emperor of the Romans, nor indeed against any other man, but only against the God whom the Christians reverence. For when in the first invasion he retired, after failing to capture Edessa[21], both he and the Magi, since they had been worsted by the God of the Christians, fell into a great dejection. Wherefore Chosroes, seeking to allay it, uttered a threat in the palace that he would make slaves of all the inhabitants of Edessa and bring them to the land of Persia, and would turn the city into a pasture for sheep. Accordingly when he had approached the city of Edessa with his whole army, he sent some of the Huns who were following him against that portion of the fortifications of the city which is above the hippodrome, with the purpose of doing no further injury than seizing the flocks which the shepherds had stationed there along the wall in great numbers: for they were confident in the strength of the place, since it was exceedingly steep, and supposed that the enemy would never dare to come so very close to the wall. So the barbarians were already laying hold of the sheep, and the shepherds were trying most valiantly to prevent them. And when a great number of Persians had come to the assistance of the Huns, the barbarians succeeded in detaching something of a flock from there, but Roman soldiers and some of the populace made a sally upon the enemy and the battle became a hand-to-hand struggle; meanwhile the flock of its own accord returned again to the shepherds. Now one of the Huns who was fighting before the others was making more trouble for the Romans than all the rest. And some rustic made a good shot and hit him on the right knee with a sling, and he immediately fell headlong from his horse to the ground, which thing heartened the Romans still more. And the battle which had begun early in the morning ended at midday, and both sides withdrew from the engagement thinking that they had the advantage. So the Romans went inside the fortifications, while the barbarians pitched their tents and made camp in a body about seven stades from the city.

Then Chosroes either saw some vision or else the thought occurred to him that if, after making two attempts, he should not be able to capture Edessa, he would thereby cover himself with much disgrace. Accordingly he decided to sell his withdrawal to the citizens of Edessa for a great sum of money. On the following day, therefore, Paulus the interpreter came along by the wall and said that some of the Roman notables should be sent to Chosroes. And they with all speed chose out four of their illustrious men and sent them. When these men reached the Median camp, they were met according to the king's order by Zaberganes, who first terrified them with many threats and then enquired of them which course was the more desirable for them, whether that leading to peace, or that leading to war. And when the envoys agreed that they would choose peace rather than the dangers of war, Zaberganes replied: "Therefore it is necessary for you to purchase this for a great sum of money." And the envoys said that they would give as much as they had provided before, when he came against them after capturing Antioch. And Zaberganes dismissed them with laughter, telling them to deliberate most carefully concerning their safety and then to come again to the Persians. And a little later Chosroes summoned them, and when they came before him, he recounted how many Roman towns he had previously enslaved and in what manner he had accomplished it; then he threatened that the inhabitants of Edessa would receive more direful treatment at the hands of the Persians, unless they should give them all the wealth which they had inside the fortifications; for only on this condition, he said, would the army depart. When the envoys heard this, they agreed that they would purchase peace from Chosroes, if only he would not prescribe impossible conditions for them: but the outcome of a conflict, they said, was plainly seen by no one at all before the struggle. For there was never a war whose outcome might be taken for granted by those who waged it. Thereupon Chosroes in anger commanded the envoys to be gone with all speed.

On the eighth day of the siege he formed the design of erecting an artificial hill against the circuit wall of the city; accordingly he cut down trees in great numbers from the adjacent districts and, without removing the leaves, laid them together in a square before the wall, at a point which no missile from the city could reach; then he heaped an immense amount of earth right upon the trees and above that threw on a great quantity of stones, not such as are suitable for building, but cut at random, and only calculated to raise the hill as quickly as possible to a great height. And he kept laying on long timbers in the midst of the earth and the stones, and made them serve to bind the structure together, in order that as it became high it should not be weak. But Peter, the Roman general (for he happened to be there with Martinus and Peranius), wishing to check the men who were engaged in this work, sent some of the Huns who were under his command against them. And they, by making a sudden attack, killed a great number; and one of the guardsmen, Argek by name, surpassed all others, for he alone killed twenty-seven. From that time on, however, the barbarians kept a careful guard, and there was no further opportunity for anyone to go out against them. But when the artisans engaged in this work, as they moved forward, came within range of missiles, then the Romans offered a most vigorous resistance from the city wall, using both their slings and their bows against them. Wherefore the barbarians devised the following plan. They provided screens of goat's hair cloth, of the kind which are called Cilician, making them of adequate thickness and height, and attached them to long pieces of wood which they always set before those who were working on the "agesta"[22] (for thus the Romans used to call in the Latin tongue the thing which they were making). Behind this neither ignited arrows nor any other weapon could reach the workmen, but all of them were thrown back by the screens and stopped there. And then the Romans, falling into a great fear, sent the envoys to Chosroes in great trepidation, and with them Stephanus, a physician of marked learning among those of his time at any rate, who also had once cured Cabades, the son of Perozes, when ill, and had been made master of great wealth by him. He, therefore, coming into the presence of Chosroes with the others, spoke as follows: "It has been agreed by all from of old that kindness is the mark of a good king. Therefore, most mighty King, while busying thyself with murders and battles and the enslavement of cities it will perhaps be possible for thee to win the other names, but thou wilt never by any means have the reputation of being 'good.' And yet least of all cities should Edessa suffer any adversity at thy hand. For there was I born, who, without any foreknowledge of what was coming to pass, fostered thee from childhood and counselled thy father to appoint thee his successor in the kingdom, so that to thee I have proved the chief cause of the kingship of Persia, but to my fatherland of her present woes. For men, as a general thing, bring down upon their own heads the most of the misfortunes which are going to befall them. But if any remembrance of such benefaction comes to thy mind, do us no further injury, and grant me this requital, by which, O King, thou wilt escape the reputation of being most cruel." Such were the words of Stephanus. But Chosroes declared that he would not depart from there until the Romans should deliver to him Peter and Peranius, seeing that, being his hereditary slaves, they had dared to array themselves against him. And if it was not their pleasure to do this, the Romans must choose one of two alternatives, either to give the Persians five hundred centenaria of gold, or to receive into the city some of his associates who would search out all the money, both gold and silver, as much as was there, and bring it to him, allowing everything else to remain in the possession of the present owners. Such then were the words which Chosroes hurled forth, being in hopes of capturing Edessa with no trouble. And the ambassadors (since all the conditions which he had announced to them seemed impossible), in despair and great vexation, proceeded to the city. And when they had come inside the city-wall, they reported the message from Chosroes, and the whole city was filled with tumult and lamentation.

Now the artificial hill was rising to a great height and was being pushed forward with much haste. And the Romans, being at a loss what to do, again sent off the envoys to Chosroes. And when they had arrived in the enemy's camp, and said that they had come to make entreaty concerning the same things, they did not even gain a hearing of any kind from the Persians, but they were insulted and driven out from there with a great tumult, and so returned to the city. At first, then, the Romans tried to over-top the wall opposite the hill by means of another structure. But since the Persian work was already rising far above even this, they stopped their building and persuaded Martinus to make the arrangements for a settlement in whatever way he wished. He then came up close to the enemy's camp and began to converse with some of the Persian commanders. But they, completely deceiving Martinus, said that their king was desirous of peace, but that he was utterly unable to persuade the Roman Emperor to have done with his strife with Chosroes and to establish peace with him at last. And they mentioned as evidence of this the fact that Belisarius, who in power and dignity was far superior to Martinus, as even he himself would not deny, had recently persuaded the king of the Persians, when he was in the midst of Roman territory, to withdraw from there into Persia, promising that envoys from Byzantium would come to him at no distant time and establish peace securely, but that he had done none of the things agreed upon, since he had found himself unable to overcome the determination of the Emperor Justinian.

XXVII

In the meantime the Romans were busying themselves as follows: They made a tunnel from the city underneath the enemy's embankment, commanding the diggers not to leave this work until they should get under the middle of the hill. By this means they were planning to burn the embankment. But as the tunnel advanced to about the middle of the hill, a sound of blows, as it were, came to the ears of those Persians who were standing above. And perceiving what was being done, they too began from above and dug on both sides of the middle, so that they might catch the Romans who were doing the damage there. But the Romans found it out and abandoned this attempt, throwing earth into the place which had been hollowed out, and then began to work on the lower part of the embankment at the end which was next to the wall, and by taking out timbers and stones and earth they made an open space just like a chamber; then they threw in there dry trunks of trees of the kind which burn most easily, and saturated them with oil of cedar and added quantities of sulphur and bitumen. So, then, they were keeping these things in readiness; and meanwhile the Persian commanders in frequent meetings with Martinus were carrying on conversations with him in the same strain as the one I have mentioned, making it appear that they would receive proposals in regard to peace. But when at last their hill had been completed, and had been raised to a great elevation, approaching the circuit-wall of the city and rising far above it in height, then they sent Martinus away, definitely refusing to arrange the treaty, and they intended from then on to devote themselves to active warfare.

Accordingly the Romans straightway set fire to the tree-trunks which had been prepared for this purpose. But when the fire had burned only a certain portion of the embankment, and had not yet been able to penetrate through the whole mass, the wood was already entirely exhausted. But they kept throwing fresh wood into the pit, not slackening their efforts for a moment. And when the fire was already active throughout the whole embankment, some smoke appeared at night rising from every part of the hill, and the Romans, who were not yet willing to let the Persians know what was being done, resorted to the following device: They filled small pots with coals and fire and threw these and also ignited arrows in great numbers to all parts of the embankment. And the Persians who were keeping guard there, began to go about in great haste and extinguish these, and they supposed that the smoke arose from them. But since the trouble increased, the barbarians rushed up to help in great numbers, and the Romans, shooting them from the wall, killed many. And Chosroes too came there about sunrise, followed by the greater part of the army, and, upon mounting the hill, he first perceived what the trouble was. For he disclosed the fact that the cause of the smoke was underneath, not in the missiles which the enemy were hurling, and he ordered the whole army to come to the rescue with all speed. And the Romans, taking courage, began to insult them, while the barbarians were at work, some throwing on earth, and others water, where the smoke appeared, hoping thus to get the better of the trouble; however, they were absolutely unable to accomplish anything. For where the earth was thrown on, the smoke, as was natural, was checked at that place, but not long afterwards it rose from another place, since the fire compelled it to force its way out wherever it could. And where the water fell most plentifully it only succeeded in making the bitumen and the sulphur much more active, and caused them to exert their full force upon the wood near by; and it constantly drove the fire forward, since the water could not penetrate inside the embankment in a quantity at all sufficient to extinguish the flame by its abundance. And in the late afternoon the smoke became so great in volume that it was visible to the inhabitants of Carrhae and to some others who dwelt far beyond them. And since a great number of Persians and of Romans had gone up on top of the embankment, a fight took place and a hand-to-hand struggle to drive each other off, and the Romans were victorious. Then even the flames rose and appeared clearly above the embankment, and the Persians abandoned this undertaking.

On the sixth day after this, at early dawn, they made an assault secretly upon a certain part of the circuit-wall with ladders, at the point which is called the Fort. And since the Romans who were keeping guard there were sleeping a quiet, peaceful sleep, as the night was drawing to its close, they silently set the ladders against the wall and were already ascending. But one of the rustics alone among the Romans happened to be awake, and he with a shout and a great noise began to rouse them all. And a hard struggle ensued in which the Persians were worsted, and they retired to their camp, leaving the ladders where they were; these the Romans drew up at their leisure. But Chosroes about midday sent a large part of the army against the so-called Great Gate in order to storm the wall. And the Romans went out and confronted them, not only soldiers, but even rustics and some of the populace, and they conquered the barbarians in battle decisively and turned them to flight. And while the Persians were still being pursued, Paulus, the interpreter, came from Chosroes, and going into the midst of the Romans, he reported that Rhecinarius had come from Byzantium to arrange the peace; and thus the two armies separated. Now it was already some days since

Rhecinarius had arrived at the camp of the barbarians. But the Persians had by no means disclosed this fact to the Romans, plainly awaiting the outcome of the attempts upon the wall which they had planned, in order that, if they should be able to capture it, they might seem in no way to be violating the treaty, while if defeated, as actually happened, they might draw up the treaty at the invitation of the Romans. And when Rhecinarius had gone inside the gates, the Persians demanded that those who were to arrange the peace should come to Chosroes without any delay, but the Romans said that envoys would be sent three days later; for that just at the moment their general, Martinus, was unwell.

And Chosroes, suspecting that the reason was not a sound one, prepared for battle. And at that time he only threw a great mass of bricks upon the embankment; but two days later he came against the fortifications of the city with the whole army to storm the wall. And at every gate he stationed some of the commanders and a part of the army, encircling the whole wall in this way, and he brought up ladders and war-engines against it. And in the rear he placed all the Saracens with some of the Persians, not in order to assault the wall, but in order that, when the city was captured, they might gather in the fugitives and catch them as in a drag-net. Such, then, was the purpose of Chosroes in arranging the army in this way. And the fighting began early in the morning, and at first the Persians had the advantage. For they were in great numbers and fighting against a very small force, since the most of the Romans had not heard what was going on and were utterly unprepared. But as the conflict advanced the city became full of confusion and tumult, and the whole population, even women and little children, were going up on to the wall. Now those who were of military age together with the soldiers were repelling the enemy most vigorously, and many of the rustics made a remarkable shew of valorous deeds against the barbarians. Meanwhile the women and children, and the aged also, were gathering stones for the fighters and assisting them in other ways. Some also filled numerous basins with olive-oil, and after heating them over fire a sufficient time everywhere along the wall, they sprinkled the oil, while boiling fiercely, upon the enemy who were assailing the wall, using a sort of whisk for the purpose, and in this way harassed them still more. The Persians, therefore, soon gave up and began to throw down their arms, and coming before the king, said that they were no longer able to hold out in the struggle. But Chosroes, in a passion of anger, drove them all on with threats and urged them forward against the enemy. And the soldiers with much shouting and tumult brought up the towers and the other engines of war to the wall and set the ladders against it, in order to capture the city with one grand rush. But since the Romans were hurling great numbers of missiles and exerting all their strength to drive them off, the barbarians were turned back by force; and as Chosroes withdrew, the Romans taunted him, inviting him to come and storm the wall. Only Azarethes at the so-called Soinian Gate was still fighting with his men, at the place which they call Tripurgia[23]. And since the Romans at this point were not a match for them, but were giving way before their assaults, already the outer wall, which they call an outwork, had been torn down by the barbarians in many places, and they were pressing most vigorously upon those who were defending themselves from the great circuit-wall; but at last Peranius with a large number of soldiers and some of the citizens went out against them and defeated them in battle and drove them off. And the assault which had begun early in the morning ended in the late afternoon, and both sides remained quiet that night, the Persians fearing for their defences and for themselves, and the Romans gathering stones and taking them to the parapets and putting everything else in complete readiness, so as to fight against the enemy on the morrow when they should attack the wall. Now on the succeeding day not one of the barbarians came against the fortifications; but on the day after that a portion of the army, urged on by Chosroes, made an assault upon the so-called Gate of Barlaus; but the Romans sallied forth and confronted them, and the Persians were decisively beaten in the engagement, and after a short time retired to the camp. And then Paulus, the interpreter of the Persians, came along by the wall and called for Martinus, in order that he might make the arrangements for the truce. Thus Martinus came to conference with the commanders of the Persians, and they concluded an agreement, by which Chosroes received five centenaria from the inhabitants of Edessa, and left them, in writing, the promise not to inflict any further injury upon the Romans; then, after setting fire to all his defences, he returned homeward with his whole army.

XXVIII

At about this time two generals of the Romans died, Justus, the nephew of the emperor, and Peranius, the Iberian, of whom the former succumbed to disease, while Peranius fell from his horse in hunting and suffered a fatal rupture. The emperor therefore appointed others in their places, dispatching Marcellus, his own nephew who was just arriving at the age of manhood, and Constantianus, who a little earlier had been sent as an envoy with Sergius to Chosroes. Then the Emperor Justinian sent Constantianus and Sergius a second time to Chosroes to arrange the truce. And they overtook him in Assyria, at the place where there are two towns, Seleucia and Ctesiphon, built by the Macedonians who after Alexander, the son of Philip, ruled over the Persians and the other nations there. These two towns are separated by the Tigris River only, for they have nothing else between them. There the envoys met Chosroes, and they demanded that he should give back to the Romans the country of Lazica, and establish peace with them on a thoroughly secure basis. But Chosroes said that it was not easy for them to come to terms with each other, unless they should first declare an armistice, and then should continue to go back and forth to each other without so much fear and settle their differences and make a peace which should be on a secure basis for the future. And it was necessary, he said, that in return for this continued armistice the Roman Emperor should give him money and should also send a certain physician, Tribunus by name, in order to spend some specified time with him. For it happened that this physician at a former time had rid him of a severe disease, and as a result of this he was especially beloved and greatly missed by him. When the Emperor Justinian heard this, he immediately sent both Tribunus and the money, amounting to twenty centenaria. [545 A.D.] In this way the treaty was made between the Romans and the Persians for five years, in the nineteenth year of the reign of the Emperor Justinian.

And a little later Arethas and Alamoundaras, the rulers of the Saracens, waged a war against each other by themselves, unaided either by the Romans or the Persians. And Alamoundaras captured one of the sons of Arethas in a sudden raid while he was pasturing horses, and straightway sacrificed him to Aphrodite; and from this it was known that Arethas was not betraying the Romans to the Persians. Later they both came together in battle with their whole armies, and the forces of Arethas were overwhelmingly victorious, and turning their enemy to flight, they killed many of them. And Arethas came within a little of capturing alive two of the sons of Alamoundaras; however, he did not actually succeed. Such, then, was the course of events among the Saracens.

But it became clear that Chosroes, the Persian king, had made the truce with the Romans with treacherous intent, in order that he might find them remiss on account of the peace and inflict upon them some grave injury. For in the third year of the truce he devised the following schemes. There were in Persia two brothers, Phabrizus and Isdigousnas, both holding most important offices there and at the same time reckoned to be the basest of all the Persians, and having a great reputation for their cleverness and evil ways. Accordingly, since Chosroes had formed the purpose of capturing the city of Daras by a sudden stroke, and to move all the Colchians out of Lazica and establish in their place Persian settlers, he selected these two men to assist him in both undertakings. For it seemed to him that it would be a lucky stroke and a really important achievement to win for himself the land of Colchis and to have it in secure possession, reasoning that this would be advantageous to the Persian empire in many ways. In the first place they would have Iberia in security forever afterwards, since the Iberians would not have anyone with whom, if they revolted, they might find safety; for since the most notable men of these barbarians together with their king, Gourgenes, had looked towards revolt, as I have stated in the preceding pages,[24] the Persians from that time on did not permit them to set up a king over themselves, nor were the Iberians single-minded subjects of the Persians, but there was much suspicion and distrust between them. And it was evident that the Iberians were most thoroughly dissatisfied and that they would attempt a revolution shortly if they could only seize upon some favourable opportunity. Furthermore, the Persian empire would be forever free from plunder by the Huns who lived next to Lazica, and he would send them against the Roman domains more easily and readily, whenever he should so desire. For he considered that, as regards the barbarians dwelling in the Caucasus, Lazica was nothing else than a bulwark against them. But most of all he hoped that the subjugation of Lazica would afford this advantage to the Persians, that starting from there they might overrun with no trouble both by land and by sea the countries along the Euxine Sea, as it is called, and thus win over the Cappadocians and the Galatians and Bithynians who adjoin them, and capture Byzantium by a sudden assault with no one opposing them. For these reasons, then, Chosroes was anxious to gain possession of Lazica, but in the Lazi he had not the least confidence. For since the time when the Romans had withdrawn from Lazica, the common people of the country naturally found the Persian rule burdensome. For the Persians are beyond all other men singular in their ways, and they are excessively rigid as regards the routine of daily life. And their laws are difficult of access for all men, and their requirements quite unbearable. But in comparison with the Lazi the difference of their thinking and living shews itself in an altogether exceptional degree, since the Lazi are Christians of the most thorough-going kind, while all the Persian views regarding religion are the exact opposite of theirs. And apart from this, salt is produced nowhere in Lazica, nor indeed does grain grow there nor the vine nor any other good thing. But from the Romans along the coast everything is brought in to them by ship, and even so they do not pay gold to the traders, but hides and slaves and whatever else happens to be found there in great abundance; and when they were excluded from this trade, they were, as was to be expected, in a state of constant vexation. When, therefore, Chosroes perceived this, he was eager to anticipate with certainty any move on their part to revolt against him. And upon considering the matter, it seemed to him to be the most advantageous course to put Goubazes, the king of the Lazi, out of the way as quickly as possible, and to move the Lazi in a body out of the country, and then to colonize this land with Persians and certain other nations.

When Chosroes had matured these plans, he sent Isdigousnas to Byzantium, ostensibly to act as an envoy, and he picked out five hundred of the most valorous of the Persians and sent them with him, directing them to get inside the city of Daras, and to take their lodgings in many different houses, and at night to set these all on fire, and, while all the Romans were occupied with this fire, as was natural, to open the gates immediately, and receive the rest of the Persian army into the city. For word had been sent previously to the commander of the city of Nisibis to conceal a large force of soldiers near by and hold them in readiness. For in this way Chosroes thought that they would destroy all the Romans with no trouble, and seizing the city of Daras, would hold it securely. But someone who knew well what was being arranged, a Roman who had come to the Persians as a deserter a little earlier, told everything to George, who was staying there at the time; now this was the same man whom I mentioned in the preceding pages[25] as having persuaded the Persians who were besieged in the fortress of Sisauranon to surrender themselves to the Romans. George therefore met this ambassador at the boundary line between Roman and Persian soil and said that this thing he was doing was not after the fashion of an embassy, and that never had so numerous a body of Persians stopped for the night in a city of the Romans. For he ought, he said, to have left behind all the rest in the town of Ammodios, and must himself enter the city of Daras with some few men. Now Isdigousnas was indignant and appeared to take it ill, because he had been insulted wrongfully, in spite of the fact that he was dispatched on an embassy to the Roman emperor. But George, paying no heed to him in his fury, saved the city for the Romans. For he received Isdigousnas into the city with only twenty men.

So having failed in this attempt, the barbarian came to Byzantium as if on an embassy, bringing with him his wife and two daughters (for this was his pretext for the crowd which had been gathered about him); but when he came before the emperor, he was unable to say anything great or small about any serious matter, although he wasted no less than ten months in Roman territory. However, he gave the emperor the gifts from Chosroes, as is customary, and a letter, in which Chosroes requested the Emperor Justinian to send word whether he was enjoying the best possible health. Nevertheless the Emperor Justinian received this Isdigousnas with more friendliness and treated him with greater honour than any of the other ambassadors of whom we know. So true was this that, whenever he entertained him, he caused Braducius, who followed him as interpreter, to recline with him on the couch, a thing which had never before happened in all time. For no one ever saw an interpreter become a table-companion of even one of the more humble officials, not to speak of a king. But he both received and dismissed this man in a style more splendid than that which befits an ambassador, although he had undertaken the embassy for no serious business, as I have said. For if anyone should count up the money expended and the gifts which Isdigousnas carried with him when he went away, he will find them amounting to more than ten centenaria of gold. So the plot against the city of Daras ended in this way for Chosroes.

XXIX

His first move against Lazica was as follows. He sent into the country a great amount of lumber suitable for the construction of ships, explaining to no one what his purpose was in so doing, but ostensibly he was sending it in order to set up engines of war on the fortifications of Petra. Next he chose out three hundred able warriors of the Persians, and sent them there under command of Phabrizus, whom I have lately mentioned, ordering him to make away with Goubazes as secretly as possible; as for the rest, he himself would take care. Now when this lumber had been conveyed to Lazica, it happened that it was struck suddenly by lightning and reduced to ashes. And Phabrizus, upon arriving in Lazica with the three hundred, began to contrive so that he might carry out the orders received by him from Chosroes regarding Goubazes. Now it happened that one of the men of note among the Colchians, Pharsanses by name, had quarrelled with Goubazes and in consequence had become exceedingly hostile to him, and now he did not dare at all to go into the presence of the king. When this was learned by Phabrizus, he summoned Pharsanses and in a conference with him disclosed the whole project, and enquired of the man in what way he ought to go about the execution of the deed. And it seemed best to them after deliberating together that Phabrizus should go into the city of Petra, and should summon Goubazes there, in order to announce to him what the king had decided concerning the interests of the Lazi. But Pharsanses secretly revealed to Goubazes what was being prepared. He, accordingly, did not come to Phabrizus at all, but began openly to plan a revolt. Then Phabrizus commanded the other Persians to attend as carefully as they could to the guarding of Petra, and to make everything as secure as possible against a siege, and he himself with the three hundred returned homeward without having accomplished his purpose. And Goubazes reported to the Emperor Justinian the condition in which they were, and begged him to grant forgiveness for what the Lazi had done in the past, and to come to their defence with all his strength, since they desired to be rid of the Median rule. For if left by themselves the Colchians would not be able to repel the power of the Persians.

[549 A.D.] When the Emperor Justinian heard this, he was overjoyed, and sent seven thousand men under the leadership of Dagisthaeus and a thousand Tzani to the assistance of the Lazi. And when this force reached the land of Colchis, they encamped together with Goubazes and the Lazi about the fortifications of Petra and commenced a siege. But since the Persians who were there made a most stalwart defence from the wall, it came about that much time was spent in the siege; for the Persians had put away an ample store of victuals in the town. And Chosroes, being greatly disturbed by these things, dispatched a great army of horse and foot against the besiegers, putting Mermeroes in command of them. And when Goubazes learned of this, he considered the matter together with Dagisthaeus and acted in the manner which I shall presently set forth.

The river Boas rises close to the territory of the Tzani among the Armenians who dwell around Pharangium. And at first its course inclines to the right for a great distance, and its stream is small and can be forded by anyone with no trouble as far as the place where the territory of the Iberians lies on the right, and the end of the Caucasus lies directly opposite. In that place many nations have their homes, and among them the Alani and Abasgi, who are Christians and friends of the Romans from of old; also the Zechi, and after them the Huns who bear the name Sabeiri. But when this river reaches the point which marks the termination of the Caucasus and of Iberia as well, there other waters also are added to it and it becomes much larger and from there flows on bearing the name of Phasis instead of Boas[26]; and it becomes a navigable stream as far as the so-called Euxine Sea into which it empties; and on either side of it lies Lazica. Now on the right of the stream particularly the whole country for a great distance is populated by the people of Lazica as far as the boundary of Iberia. For all the villages of the Lazi are here beyond the river, and towns have been built there from of old, among which are Archaeopolis, a very strong place, and Sebastopolis, and the fortress of Pitius, and Scanda and Sarapanis over against the boundary of Iberia. Moreover there are two cities of the greatest importance in that region, Rhodopolis and Mocheresis. But on the left of the river, while the country belongs to Lazica as far as one day's journey for an unencumbered traveller, the land is without human habitation. Adjoining this land is the home of the Romans who are called Pontic. Now it was in the territory of Lazica, in the part which was altogether uninhabited, that the Emperor Justinian founded the city of Petra in my own time. This was the place where John, surnamed Tzibus, established the monopoly, as I have told in the previous narrative[27], and gave cause to the Lazi to revolt. And as one leaves the city of Petra going southward, the Roman territory commences immediately, and there are populous towns there, and one which bears the name of Rhizaeum, also Athens and certain others as far as Trapezus. Now when the Lazi brought in Chosroes, they crossed the River Boas and came to Petra keeping the Phasis on the right, because, as they said, they would thus provide against being compelled to spend much time and trouble in ferrying the men across the River Phasis, but in reality they did not wish to display their own homes to the Persians. And yet Lazica is everywhere difficult to traverse both to the right and to the left of the River Phasis. For there are on both sides of the river exceedingly high and jagged mountains, and as a result the passes are narrow and very long. (The Romans call the roads through such passes "clisurae" when they put their own word into a Greek form.[28]) But since at that time Lazica happened to be unguarded, the Persians had reached Petra very easily with the Lazi who were their guides.

But on this occasion Goubazes, upon learning of the advance of the Persians, directed Dagisthaeus to send some men to guard with all their strength the pass which is below the River Phasis, and he bade him not on any account to abandon the siege until they should be able to capture Petra and the Persians in it. He himself meanwhile with the whole Colchian army came to the frontier of Lazica, in order to devote all his strength to guarding the pass there. Now it happened that long before he had persuaded the Alani and Sabeiri to form an alliance with him, and they had agreed for three centenaria not merely to assist the Lazi in guarding the land from plunder, but also to render Iberia so destitute of men that not even the Persians would be able to come in from there in the future. And Goubazes had promised that the emperor would give them this money. So he reported the agreement to the Emperor Justinian and besought him to send this money for the barbarians and afford the Lazi some consolation in their great distress. He also stated that the treasury owed him his salary for ten years, for though he was assigned a post among the privy counsellors in the palace, he had received no payment from it since the time when Chosroes came into the land of Colchis. And the Emperor Justinian intended to fulfil this request, but some business came up to occupy his attention and he did not send the money at the proper time. So Goubazes was thus engaged.

But Dagisthaeus, being a rather young man and by no means competent to carry on a war against Persia, did not handle the situation properly. For while he ought to have sent certainly the greater part of the army to the pass, and perhaps should have assisted in person in this enterprise, he sent only one hundred men, just as if he were managing a matter of secondary importance. He himself, moreover, though besieging Petra with the whole army, accomplished nothing, although the enemy were few. For while they had been at the beginning not less than fifteen hundred, they had been shot at by Romans and Lazi in their fighting at the wall for a long time, and had made a display of valour such as no others known to us have made, so that many were falling constantly and they were reduced to an exceedingly small number. So while the Persians, plunged in despair and at a loss what to do, were remaining quiet, the Romans made a trench along the wall for a short space, and the circuit-wall at this point fell immediately. But it happened that inside this space there was a building which did not stand back at all from the circuit-wall, and this reached to the whole length of the fallen portion; thus, taking the place of the wall for the besieged, it rendered them secure none the less. But this was not sufficient greatly to disturb the Romans. For knowing well that by doing the same thing elsewhere they would capture the city with the greatest ease, they became still more hopeful than before. For this reason Dagisthaeus sent word to the emperor of what had come to pass, and proposed that prizes of victory should be in readiness for him, indicating what rewards the emperor should bestow upon himself and his brother; for he would capture Petra after no great time. So the Romans and the Tzani made a most vigorous assault upon the wall, but the Persians unexpectedly withstood them, although only a very few were left. And since the Romans were accomplishing nothing by assaulting the wall, they again turned to digging. And they went so far in this work that the foundations of the circuit-wall were no longer on solid ground, but stood for the most part over empty space, and, in the nature of things, would fall almost immediately. And if Dagisthaeus had been willing immediately to apply fire to the foundations, I think that the city would have been captured by them straightway; but, as it was, he was awaiting encouragement from the emperor, and so, always hesitating and wasting time, he remained inactive. Such, then, was the course of events in the Roman camp.

XXX

But Mermeroes, after passing the Iberian frontier with the whole Median army, was moving forward with the River Phasis on his right. For he was quite unwilling to go through the country of Lazica, lest any obstacle should confront him there. For he was eager to save the city of Petra and the Persians in it, even though a portion of the circuit-wall had fallen down suddenly. For it had been hanging in the air, as I have said; and volunteers from the Roman army to the number of fifty got inside the city, and raised the shout proclaiming the Emperor Justinian triumphant. These men were led by a young man of Armenian birth, John by name, the son of Thomas whom they used to call by the surname Gouzes. This Thomas had built many of the strongholds about Lazica at the direction of the emperor, and he commanded the soldiers there, seeming to the emperor an intelligent person. Now John, when the Persians joined battle with his men, was wounded and straightway withdrew to the camp with his followers, since no one else of the Roman army came to support him. Meanwhile the Persian Mirranes who commanded the garrison in Petra, fearing for the city, directed all the Persians to keep guard with the greatest diligence, and he himself went to Dagisthaeus, and addressed him with fawning speeches and deceptive words, agreeing readily to surrender the city not long afterwards. In this way he succeeded in deceiving him so that the Roman army did not immediately enter the city.

Now when the army of Mermeroes came to the pass, the Roman garrison, numbering one hundred men, confronted them there and offered a stalwart resistance, and they held in check their opponents who were attempting the entrance. But the Persians by no means withdrew, but those who fell were constantly replaced by others, and they kept advancing, trying with all their strength to force their way in. Among the Persians more than a thousand perished, but at last the Romans were worn out with killing, and, being forced back by the throng, they withdrew, and running up to the heights of the mountain there were saved. Dagisthaeus, upon learning this, straightway abandoned the siege without giving any commands to the army, and proceeded to the River Phasis; and all the Romans followed him, leaving their possessions behind in the camp. And when the Persians observed what was being done, they opened their gates and came forth, and approached the tents of the enemy in order to capture the camp. But the Tzani, who had not followed after Dagisthaeus, as it happened, rushed out to defend the camp, and they routed the enemy without difficulty and killed many. So the Persians fled inside their fortifications, and the Tzani, after plundering the Roman camp proceeded straight for Rhizaeum. And from there they came to Athens and betook themselves to their homes through the territory of the Trapezuntines.

And Mermeroes and the Median army came there on the ninth day after the withdrawal of Dagisthaeus; and in the city they found left of the Persian garrison three hundred and fifty men wounded and unfit for fighting, and only one hundred and fifty men unhurt; for all the rest had perished. Now the survivors had in no case thrown the bodies of the fallen outside the fortifications, but though stifled by the evil stench, they held out in a manner beyond belief, in order that they might not afford the enemy any encouragement for the prosecution of the siege, by letting them know that most of their number had perished. And Mermeroes remarked by way of a taunt that the Roman state was worthy of tears and lamentation, because they had come to such a state of weakness that they had been unable by any device to capture one hundred and fifty Persians without a wall. And he was eager to build up the portions of the circuit-wall which had fallen down; but since at the moment he had neither lime nor any of the other necessary materials for the building ready at hand, he devised the following plan. Filling with sand the linen bags in which the Persians had carried their provisions into the land of Colchis, he laid them in the place of the stones, and the bags thus arranged took the place of the wall. And choosing out three thousand of his able fighting men, he left them there, depositing with them victuals for no great length of time, and commanding them to attend to the building of the fortifications; then he himself with all the rest of the army turned back and marched away.

But since, if he went from there by the same road, no means of provisioning his army was available, since he had left everything in Petra which had been brought in by the army from Iberia, he planned to go by another route through the mountains, where he learned that the country was inhabited, in order that by foraging there he might be able to live off the land. In the course of this journey one of the notables among the Lazi, Phoubelis by name, laid an ambush for the Persians while camping for the night, bringing with him Dagisthaeus with two thousand of the Romans; and these men, making a sudden attack, killed some of the Persians who were grazing their horses, and after securing the horses as plunder they shortly withdrew. Thus, then, Mermeroes with the Median army departed from there.

But Goubazes, upon learning what had befallen the Romans both at Petra and at the pass, did not even so become frightened, nor did he give up the guarding of the pass where he was, considering that their hope centred in that place. For he understood that, even if the Persians had been able by forcing back the Romans on the left of the River Phasis to cross over the pass and get into Petra, they could thereby inflict no injury upon the land of the Lazi, since they were utterly unable to cross the Phasis, in particular because no ships were at their disposal. For in depth this river is not inferior to the deepest rivers, and it spreads out to a great width. Moreover it has such a strong current that when it empties into the sea, it goes on as a separate stream for a very great distance, without mingling at all with the sea-water. Indeed, those who navigate in those parts are able to draw up drinking water in the midst of the sea. Moreover, the Lazi have erected fortresses all along the right bank of the river, in order that, even when the enemy are ferried across in boats, they may not be able to disembark on the land.

The Emperor Justinian at this time sent to the nation of the Sabeiri the money which had been agreed upon, and he rewarded Goubazes and the Lazi with additional sums of money. And it happened that long before this time he had sent another considerable army also to Lazica, which had not yet arrived there. The commander of this army was Rhecithancus, from Thrace, a man of discretion and a capable warrior. Such then was the course of these events.

Now when Mermeroes got into the mountains, as I have said, he was anxious to fill Petra with provisions from there. For he did not by any means think that the victuals which they had brought in with them would suffice for the garrison there, amounting to three thousand men. But since the supplies they found along the way barely sufficed for the provisioning of that army, which numbered no less than thirty thousand, and since on this account they were able to send nothing at all of consequence to Petra, upon consideration he found it better for them that the greater part of the army should depart from the land of Colchis, and that some few should remain there, who were to convey to the garrison in Petra the most of the provisions which they might find, while using the rest to maintain themselves comfortably. He therefore selected five thousand men and left them there, appointing as commanders over them Phabrizus and three others. For it seemed to him unnecessary to leave more men there, since there was no enemy at all. And he himself with the rest of the army came into Persarmenia and remained quietly in the country around Doubios.

Now the five thousand, upon coming nearer to the frontier of Lazica, encamped in a body beside the Phasis River, and from there they went about in small bands and plundered the neighbouring country. Now when Goubazes perceived this, he sent word to Dagisthaeus to hasten there to his assistance: for it would be possible for them to do the enemy some great harm. And he did as directed, moving forward with the whole Roman army with the River Phasis on the left, until he came to the place where the Lazi where encamped on the opposite bank of the river. Now it happened that the Phasis could be forded at this point, a fact which neither the Romans nor the Persians suspected in the least because of their lack of familiarity with these regions; but the Lazi knew it well, and they made the crossing suddenly and joined the Roman army. And the Persians chose out a thousand men of repute among them and sent them forth, that no one might advance against the camp to harm it. And two of this force, who had gone out ahead of their fellows to reconnoitre, fell unexpectedly into the hands of the enemy and informed them of the whole situation. The Romans, therefore, and the Lazi fell suddenly upon the thousand men, and not one of them succeeded in escaping, but the most of them were slain, while some also were captured; and through these the men of Goubazes and Dagisthaeus succeeded in learning the numbers of the Median army and the length of the journey to them and the condition in which they then were. They therefore broke camp and marched against them with their whole army, calculating so that they would fall upon them well on in the night; their own force amounted to fourteen thousand men. Now the Persians, having no thought of an enemy in their minds, were enjoying a long sleep; for they supposed that the river was impassable, and that the thousand men, with no one to oppose them, were making a long march somewhere. But the Romans and Lazi at early dawn unexpectedly fell upon them, and they found some still buried in slumber and others just roused from sleep and lying defenceless upon their beds. Not one of them, therefore, thought of resistance, and the majority were caught and killed, while some also were captured by the enemy, among whom happened to be one of the commanders; only a few escaped in the darkness and were saved. And the Romans and Lazi captured the camp and all the standards, and they also secured many weapons and a great deal of money as plunder, besides great numbers of horses and mules. And pursuing them for a very great distance they came well into Iberia. There they happened upon certain others of the Persians also and slew a great number. Thus the Persians departed from Lazica; and the Romans and Lazi found there all the supplies, including great quantities of flour, which the barbarians had brought in from Iberia, in order to transport them to Petra, and they burned them all. And they left a large number of Lazi in the pass, so that it might no longer be possible for the Persians to carry in supplies to Petra, and they returned with all the plunder and the captives. [549 A.D.] And the fourth year of the truce between the Romans and Persians came to an end, being the twenty-third year of the reign of the Emperor Justinian.

And John the Cappadocian one year before this came to Byzantium at the summons of the emperor. For at that time the Empress Theodora had reached the term of her life. However, he was quite unable to recover any of his former dignities, but he continued to hold the priestly honour against his will; and yet the vision had often come to the man that he would arrive at royalty. For the divine power is accustomed to tempt those whose minds are not solidly grounded by nature, by holding before their vision, on great and lofty hopes, that which is counted splendid among men. At any rate the marvel-mongers were always predicting to this John many such imaginary things, and especially that he was bound to be clothed in the garment of Augustus. Now there was a certain priest in Byzantium, Augustus by name, who guarded the treasures of the temple of Sophia. So when John had been shorn and declared worthy of the priestly dignity by force, inasmuch as he had no garment becoming a priest, he had been compelled by those who were in charge of this business to put on the cloak and the tunic of this Augustus who was near by, and in this, I suppose, his prophecy reached its fulfilment.

FOOTNOTES

[1] That is, the Saracens subject to the Romans and those subject to the Persians.

[2] Cf. Book I. xxii. 4.

[3] The Huns placed a part of their force in the rear of the defenders of the pass, which lies between the sea and the mountains, sending them around by the same path, probably, as that used by Xerxes when he destroyed Leonidas and his three hundred Spartans; see Herod. vii. 216-218.

[4] "Secretary of secrets."

[5] Cf. Book I. xxii. 4.

[6] Cf. Book II. i. 13; iii. 47.

[7] Cf. Book I. xxii. 4.

[8] Cf. Book II. xxi. 30-32.

[9] This term was applied to the "Blue Faction" in Byzantium and elsewhere.

[10] Cf. Book I. xxii. 4.

[11] Nine MS. lines are missing at this point.

[12] Cf. Book II. x. 24.

[13] Cf. Book I. xii. 4 ff.

[14] Cf. Book I. viii. 21-22.

[15] Cf. chap. v. 31.

[16] I.e. "groin."

[17] Modern Galata.

[18] The official dress.

[19] Vesta.

[20] Cf. section 9 above.

[21] Cf. Book II. xii. 31-34.

[22] Latin agger, "mound."

[23] "Three Towers."

[24] Cf. Book I. xii. 5 ff.

[25] Book II. xix. 23.

[26] Procopius seems to have confused two separate and distinct rivers.

[27] Cf. Book II. xv. 11.

[28] Latin clausura, "a narrow shut-in road."

www.ingramcontent.com/pod-product-compliance
Lightning Source LLC
Chambersburg PA
CBHW071724040426
42446CB00011B/2213